005.369 Micro -S

teach yourself®

excel 2002

excel 2002

moira stephen

The **teach yourself** series does exactly what it says, and it works. For over 60 years, more than 40 million people have learnt over 750 subjects the **teach yourself** way, with impressive results.

be where you want to be with **teach yourself**

For UK orders: please contact Bookpoint Ltd., 130 Milton Park, Abingdon, Oxon OX14 4SB. Telephone: +44 (0)1235 827720. Fax: +44 (0)1235 400454. Lines are open 09.00–18.00, Monday to Saturday, with a 24-hour message answering service. You can also order through our website www.madaboutbooks.com.

For USA order enquiries: please contact McGraw-Hill Customer Services, PO Box 545, Blacklick, OH 43004-0545, USA. Telephone: 1-800-722-4726. Fax: 1-614-755-5645.

For Canada order enquiries: please contact McGraw-Hill Ryerson Ltd., 300 Water St, Whitby, Ontario L1N 9B6, Canada. Telephone: 905 430 5000. Fax: 905 430 5020.

Long renowned as the authoritative source for self-guided learning – with more than 30 million copies sold worldwide – the *Teach Yourself* series includes over 300 titles in the fields of languages, crafts, hobbies, business, computing and education.

British Library Cataloguing in Publication Data
A catalogue record for this title is available from The British Library.

Library of Congress Catalog Card Number: On file.

First published in UK 2003 by Hodder Headline Plc., 338 Euston Road, London, NW1 3BH.

First published in US 2003 by Contemporary Books, A Division of The McGraw-Hill Companies, 1 Prudential Plaza, 130 East Randolph Street, Chicago, Illinois 60601 USA.

The 'Teach Yourself' name and logo are registered trade marks of Hodder & Stoughton Ltd.

Copyright © 2003 Moira Stephen

In UK: All rights reserved. No part of this publication may be reproduced or transmitted in any form or by any means, electronic or mechanical, including photocopy, recording, or any information storage and retrieval system, without permission in writing from the publisher or under licence from the Copyright Licensing Agency Limited. Further details of such licences (for reprographic reproduction) may be obtained from the Copyright Licensing Agency Limited, of 90 Tottenham Court Road, London W1T 4LP.

In US: All rights reserved. Except as permitted under the United States Copyright Act of 1976, no part of this publication may be reproduced or distributed in any form or by any means, or stored in a database or retrieval system, without the prior written permission of Contemporary Books.

Typeset by MacDesign, Southampton
Printed in Great Britain for Hodder & Stoughton Educational, a division of Hodder Headline Plc, 338 Euston Road, London NW1 3BH by Cox & Wyman Ltd., Reading, Berkshire.

Impression number   10 9 8 7 6 5 4 3 2 1

Year   2007 2006 2005 2004 2003

contents

01	**getting started**	**1**
	1.1 Introducing Excel	2
	1.2 Hardware and software requirements	2
	1.3 Installing Excel	3
	1.4 Starting Excel	4
	1.5 The Excel screen	4
	1.6 Workbooks and worksheets	5
	1.7 Menus	7
	1.8 Help!	8
	1.9 Help on the Internet	15
	1.10 Exiting Excel	16
02	**basic excel skills**	**17**
	2.1 Spreadsheet jargon	18
	2.2 File handling	20
	2.3 Moving around your worksheet	23
	2.4 Selection techniques	24
	2.5 Entering text and numeric data	27
	2.6 Editing text and numeric data	28
	2.7 Column width	29
	2.8 Text wrap within a cell	31
	2.9 Number formats	33
	2.10 Formulas	34
	2.11 AutoFill	37
	2.12 Another worksheet!	39
	2.13 Move or copy cell contents	40
	2.14 Insert and delete rows and columns	42
	2.15 Print preview and print	43

03	**formatting and layout**	**46**
3.1	Bold, italic and underline	47
3.2	Alignment	48
3.3	More formatting options	49
3.4	Format Painter	52
3.5	Conditional formatting	53
3.6	Change the default font	54
3.7	Freeze panes	55
3.8	Split screen	56
3.9	Page layout	57
04	**working with sheets**	**63**
4.1	Moving between worksheets	64
4.2	Worksheet design	64
4.3	Inserting worksheets	66
4.4	Deleting worksheets	67
4.5	Renaming worksheets	68
4.6	Moving and copying worksheets	68
4.7	Grouping worksheets	69
05	**formulas and functions**	**71**
5.1	AutoSum	72
5.2	Inserting a function	76
5.3	Statistical functions	78
5.4	View formulas	80
5.5	Relative and absolute addresses	82
5.6	Circular references	86
5.7	Named ranges	87
5.8	Comments	91
5.9	Worksheet protection	93
06	**more functions**	**96**
6.1	Logical Functions	97
6.2	Statistical and Math functions	106
6.3	Text functions	107

	6.4	Date functions	110
	6.5	Financial functions	113
	6.6	Lookup functions	115
	6.7	Data tables	117
	6.8	Scenarios	120
	6.9	PivotTable	122
07	**charting and drawing**		**127**
	7.1	Preparing your data	128
	7.2	Chart Wizard	129
	7.3	A chart in your worksheet	131
	7.4	A chart on a separate sheet	134
	7.5	Charts without the Wizard	134
	7.6	Printing your chart	134
	7.7	Default chart	136
	7.8	Special effects	136
	7.9	Drawing tools	138
	7.10	Some more options	141
08	**autoformat, styles and templates**		**144**
	8.1	AutoFormat	145
	8.2	Introducing styles	146
	8.3	Working with styles	146
	8.4	Workbook templates	148
	8.5	Worksheet templates	151
09	**list management**		**153**
	9.1	Terminology	154
	9.2	Sort	155
	9.3	AutoFilter	158
	9.4	Advanced Filter	161
	9.5	Data validation	162
	9.6	Data form	164
	9.7	Subtotals	166
	9.8	Database functions	168

10 macros — 171

- 10.1 What are macros? — 172
- 10.2 Recording your macro — 173
- 10.3 Playing back your macro — 174
- 10.4 Ideas for more macros — 175
- 10.5 Deleting a macro — 177
- 10.6 Editing a macro — 178
- 10.7 Saving macros on exit — 179

11 toolbars — 181

- 11.1 Standard and Formatting toolbars — 182
- 11.2 Moving toolbars — 183
- 11.3 Showing and hiding toolbars — 183
- 11.4 Editing existing toolbars — 184
- 11.5 Creating a new toolbar — 187
- 11.6 Adding your macros to toolbars — 187
- 11.7 Change the button image and name — 188
- 11.8 Resetting toolbars — 189

12 excel with other applications — 191

- 12.1 Linking vs embedding — 192
- 12.2 Copy and Paste — 193
- 12.3 Linking data — 193
- 12.4 Embedding data — 195
- 12.5 Mail Merge — 195

13 excel and the web — 198

- 13.1 E-mail — 199
- 13.2 Hyperlinks — 201
- 13.3 Preparing a Web page — 205
- 13.4 Editing your Web page — 207
- 13.5 Publishing to the Web — 209

taking it further — 211

index — 213

In this unit you will learn

- what you need to run Excel 2002
- how to install the software
- how to start Excel
- about the Excel screen and its tools
- how to use the Help system

Aims of this chapter

This chapter introduces the spreadsheet package Excel. We will start with an overview of the package, and consider the hardware and software specifications required to run Excel successfully. We then move on to look at how you install the package on your computer. Getting into Excel, the working environment, on-line Help system and exiting Excel will also be discussed.

1.1 Introducing Excel

Excel is a very powerful spreadsheet package – but don't let that put you off! You can use Excel to produce simple spreadsheets to help you prepare your invoices, budgets and summary statements. You can also use Excel to chart your data, manipulate it using database-type features and publish your worksheet to the Web. Excel integrates well with the other packages in Microsoft Office XP and you'll find out how you can use this to your advantage. Finally, Excel is very Web orientated – you'll soon be able to hyperlink to other files and Internet addresses, send e-mails and publish your worksheets and charts on the Web!

It is assumed that you have a working knowledge of Windows.

1.2 Hardware and software requirements

The hardware and software specifications given are for Office XP.

The recommended configuration is a PC with Windows 2000 Professional, a Pentium III Processor and 128 MB of RAM.

The minimum specification is as follows:

Personal Computer	Pentium 133 MHz or higher processor
Operating System	Windows 98, Windows Me (Millennium Edition), Windows NT 4.0 with Service Pack 6 (SP6) or later, Windows 2000, or Windows XP.
RAM	Depends on the operating system used, plus 8MB for each office application in use at one time. **Windows 98**: 24 MB of RAM **Windows Me or NT**: 32 MB of RAM **Windows 2000 or XP**: 64 MB of RAM
Hard disk	Approximately 245 MB of hard disk space in total, with 115 MB on the hard disk where the operating system is installed.
CD-ROM Drive	The software is only supplied on CD
Monitor	Super VGA or higher-resolution
Mouse	Microsoft Mouse, IntelliMouse® or compatible pointing device

See http://www.microsoft.com/uk/office/evaluation/sysreqs.asp for full details of system requirements.

1.3 Installing Excel

Excel is supplied in all of the Microsoft Office XP editions.

Standard: Word, Excel, Outlook and PowerPoint.

Professional: As Standard plus Access and FrontPage.

Developer: As Professional plus Sharepoint Team Services, Developer tools.

Professional with Publisher: (only available pre-installed).

Small Business: Word, Excel, Outlook and Publisher (only available pre-installed).

These instructions are for installing Microsoft Office:

1 Insert Disk 1 into the CD-ROM drive

2 Follow the instructions on your screen

3 Repeat the process for the other disks

1.4 Starting Excel

Starting through the Shortcut Bar:

1 Click the **Excel** tool

From the Start menu:

1 Click the **Start** button on the Taskbar
2 Point to **Programs**
3 Click **Microsoft Excel**

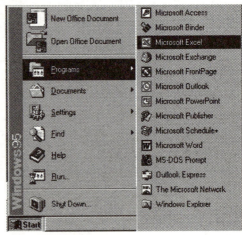

1.5 The Excel screen

Whichever method you choose to start Excel, you are presented with a new workbook displaying a blank worksheet. We'll take a tour of the Excel screen, so that you know what the various areas are called.

If the Workbook window is maximized, the Workbook and the Application windows share one Title bar containing the Application and Workbook names.

You'll find the different screen areas referred to by the names given below in the on-line Help and throughout this book.

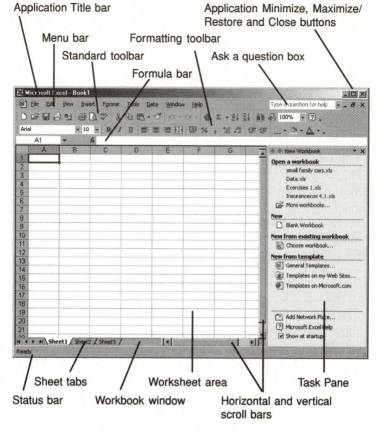

1.6 Workbooks and worksheets

When working in Excel, the files that you create and work with are called workbooks, each consisting of a number of worksheets. A worksheet is the primary document, and consists of cells organized in rows and columns. The default number of worksheets in a workbook is three, but you can add more if necessary, or remove any that you don't need.

Related data is usually best kept on separate worksheets within the same workbook – this makes it easier to find and manage your data.

For example, if you were collating regional sales figures, you could record the figures for each region on a separate sheet within the same workbook. Alternatively, you could have a separate workbook for each region and record the monthly or quarterly sales figures on separate sheets within each region's workbook.

Worksheets will be discussed more fully in Chapter 4.

Menus and toolbars

Office XP applications personalize your menus and toolbars automatically. The items that you use most often are featured on your personalized toolbars or menus.

Once you start using Excel, you'll find that the menu options most recently used will be displayed first when you open a menu (this is your personalized menu). You can expand the menus to reveal all commands (simply click on the down arrow that appears at the bottom of each menu). You may find that the menu automatically expands if you just wait once you've opened it. If you wish to modify the way that the menus work, open the View menu choose Toolbars, Customize. You can switch the *Always show full menus* or *Show full menus after a short delay* options on or off on the Options tab.

The Standard and Formatting toolbars share a single row, so that you have more room for your work (if you wish to disable the row sharing option see Chapter 11). Click the drop-down arrow to the right of a toolbar to display additional tools. The tools that you used most recently are displayed on the visible part of the toolbar on your screen.

See Chapter 11 for more information on toolbars.

Don't panic if your toolbars and menus are not exactly the same as those illustrated in this book.

Task Pane

When Excel is installed on your machine, the Task Pane for creating and opening files is set to display at Startup. This means that the Task Pane appears down the right side of the screen each time that you start Excel. You can easily close the Task Pane by clicking the Close button at the top right of it.

If you don't want the Task Pane displayed each time that you start Excel, deselect the **Show at startup** checkbox at the bottom of the pane. The next time you start Excel the Task Pane will not be displayed.

You can display the Task Pane at any time.

1 Open the **View** menu
2 Select **Task Pane**

You will encounter a number of Task Panes when working in Excel. The **Office Clipboard** Task Pane can be used when copying and moving items (see 2.13) and the **Styles and Formatting** and **Reveal Formatting** Task Panes are useful when formatting your document (see Chapter 3).

Smart tags

As you work with Excel you will notice that 'smart tags' appear at various times e.g. when you copy paste some data (see 2.13). If you click the smart tag it will display a list of options that allow you to control or customise the task that you are performing.

1.7 Menus

There are nine main menus in the Excel application Window. You can use these to access any function or feature in Excel. I suggest that you have a browse through them to get an idea of what's available – some menu items may appear familiar to you, some will be new. You can display a menu and select menu options, just as in any Windows application, using either the mouse or the keyboard.

Using the mouse

1 Click on the menu name to display the list of options available in that menu

2 Click on the menu item you wish to use

• Click the extension arrow at the bottom of your personalized menu to display all the options available.

Using the keyboard

To open a menu using the keyboard:

- Hold down the [**Alt**] key on your keyboard and press the underlined letter, e.g. [**Alt**]-[**F**] will open the File menu, [**Alt**]-[**I**] will open the Insert menu.

Each item in a menu list also has a letter underlined in it. To select an item from the menu list either:

- Press the appropriate letter on your keyboard.

Or

- Use the up and down arrow keys on your keyboard until the item you want is selected, then press the [**Enter**] key.

Once a menu list is displayed, you can press the right or left arrow keys on your keyboard to move from one menu to another.

To close a menu without selecting an item from the list:

- Click the menu name again, click anywhere off the menu list or press the [**Esc**] key on your keyboard.

In addition to the menus, many of the commands can be initiated using the toolbars, keyboard shortcuts or shortcut menus. Each of these areas will be covered as you progress through the book.

1.8 Help!

As you work with Excel you will most probably find that you come a bit unstuck from time to time and need help! There are several ways of getting help – most of them very intuitive and user-friendly.

Office Assistant

To call on the Office Assistant, press [**F1**], click the **Microsoft Excel Help** tool 🔲 on the Standard toolbar, or click Office Assistant 🔲 on the Status bar.

Depending upon what you have been doing, the Assistant may display a list of topics that might be of interest.

To choose a topic from the **What would you like to do?** list, simply click on the topic.

If you have a specific question you want to ask, type it in at the prompt and click the **Search** button.

The Assistant will display the Help page.

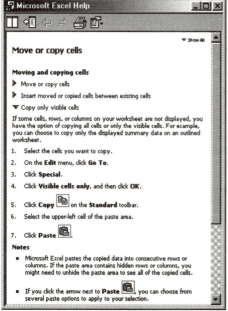

Some Help pages contain text in a different colour – usually blue. If the text is part of a list, click it to expand and collapse the Help item. If the coloured text is embedded within the main text on a page it is probably a phrase or some jargon that has an explanation or definition attached to it. Simply click the coloured text to toggle the display of the definition.

When you've finished exploring the Help system, click the **Close** button at the top right of the Help window.

The Office Assistant can remain visible as you work on your worksheet, or you can hide it and call on it as required. If you opt to leave it displayed, drag it to an area of the screen where it doesn't obscure your work.

- If you leave the Office Assistant displayed, left-click on it any time you want to ask a question.
- To hide the Office Assistant, right-click on it and choose **Hide** from the pop-up menu.

To customize the Office Assistant

You can customize the Office Assistant to take on a different appearance, or behave in a different way.

1 Show the Office Assistant (press [**F1**], click the **Help** tool or click) if required
2 Click the **Options** button
3 To change its appearance, select the **Gallery** tab and browse through the options available (use the **Next** and **Back** buttons to move through the various 'guises')

- If you find an Assistant you would like to use, click **OK**.
- To leave the Assistant as it was, click **Cancel**.

4 To change its behaviour, select the **Options** tab and set the options as required – click on an option to switch it on or off. A tick in a box means an option is selected, an empty box means it isn't.

- If you don't want to use the Office Assistant, you can switch it off on the **Options** tab – simply deselect the *Use the Office Assistant* checkbox.

5 Click **OK** to set the options selected or **Cancel** to leave things as they were

Tips

The Office Assistant is constantly monitoring your actions. If it thinks that it has a tip that may be useful to you, a light bulb will light up beside it. To read its tip, click the bulb.

Ask a question box

You can also access the Help system using the Ask a question box on the Menu bar.

Type in your question and press [**Enter**]. Choose the Help topic required from the list that is displayed – click on it.

What's This?

If you haven't used Microsoft Office products before, there will be many tools, menus, buttons and areas on your screen that puzzle you. The *What's This?* feature can help you here – it works best when a workbook is open, as most of the tools, menus and screen areas are then active.

To find out what a tool does:

1 Hold down the [**Shift**] key and press [**F1**]
2 Click the tool

To find out about an item in a menu list:

1 Hold down the [**Shift**] key and press [**F1**]
2 Open the menu list and select the option from the list

To find out about anything else within the application window:

1 Hold down the [**Shift**] key and press [**F1**]
2 Click on the item

If you accidentally invoke the *What's This* Help option, press [**Shift**]-[**F1**] (or the [**Esc**] key) to cancel it.

Contents and Index

Whether or not you opt to use the Office Assistant, the **Excel Help** tool will open the on-line Help system. You can also access the Help system from the Help menu.

If you access the Help system through the Office Assistant, the Help page requested is displayed on the screen.

You can interrogate the Help system using the Contents, the Answer Wizard or the Index tabs.

Click the tool to toggle the display of the tabs.

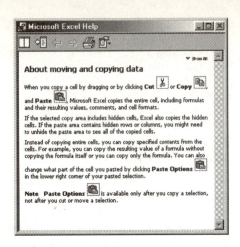

Contents tab

You can 'browse' through the Help system from the Contents tab.

Click the ⊞ to the left of a book to display or ⊟ to hide its contents. When a book is open, you will be presented with a list of topics.

To display a topic:

1 Click on it

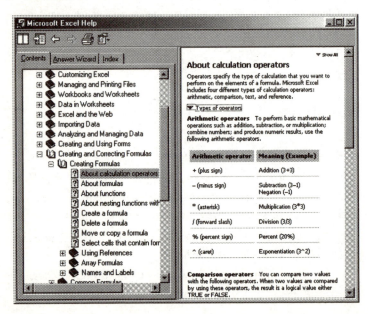

2 Work through the Help system until you find the Help you need

To print a topic:

- Click the **Print** tool in the Help window when the topic is displayed.

To revisit pages you've already been to:

- Click the **Back** tool or **Forward** tool to go back and forward through the pages.

Close the Help window when you're finished.

Answer Wizard tab

If you want to interrogate the Help system by asking a question, try the Answer Wizard tab.

1 Enter your question e.g. *How do I create a chart* and click **Search**
2 Select a topic from the *Select topic to display* list
- The Help page will be displayed.

Index tab

If you know what you are looking for, the Index tab gives you quick access to any topic and is particularly useful once you are familiar with the terminology used in Excel.

1 At the Microsoft Excel dialog box, select the **Index** tab
2 Type the word you're looking for in the *Type keywords* field and click **Search**

Or

3 Double-click on a word in the *Or choose keywords* list
4 Choose a topic from the *Choose a topic* list
5 Work through the Help system until you find what you are looking for
6 Close the Help window when you've finished

If the topics listed don't provide the answer you need, click the **Search on Web** button and send your questions to the Web Help system.

ScreenTips

If you point to any tool on a displayed toolbar, a ScreenTip will probably appear to describe the purpose of the tool.

If no ScreenTips appear, you can easily switch them on.

To switch ScreenTips on or off:

1 Point to any toolbar that is displayed and click the right mouse button
2 Choose **Customize...** from the shortcut menu
3 In the **Customize** dialog box select the **Options** tab
4 To switch the ScreenTips on, select the *Show ScreenTips on toolbars* option (deselect this option to switch them off)
5 Click **Close**

Dialog box Help

When you access a dialog box e.g. the Customize one shown below, you can get Help on any item within it that you don't understand.

To get Help on an item in a dialog box:

1 Click the **Help** button ? at the right of the title bar
2 Click on an option, button or item in the dialog box that you want explained

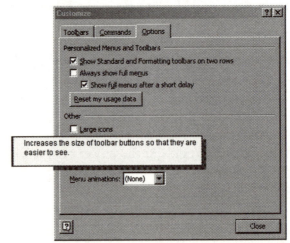

- A brief explanation of the option, button or item you click on will be displayed.

3 Click anywhere within the dialog box to cancel the explanation

1.9 Help on the Internet

If you can't find the help you are looking for in the normal Help system, visit the Microsoft Office Update Web site to get updated Help files, answers to frequently asked questions on Excel, tips, technical support and articles on Excel and Office XP.

1 Open the **Help** menu
2 Choose **Office on the Web**
3 Navigate your way through the Help pages until you find the information required

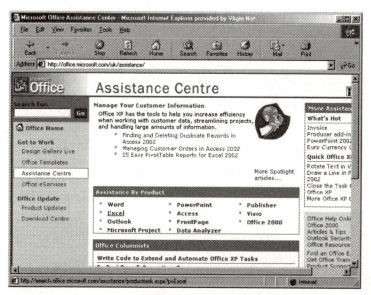

1.10 Exiting Excel

When you have finished working in Excel you must close the application down – don't just switch off your computer!

To exit Excel:

- Open the **File** menu and choose **Exit**.

Or

- Click the **Close** button ☒ in the right-hand corner of the Application Title bar.

If you have been working on a workbook, but have not saved it, you will be prompted to do so – see '*Save workbook*', 2.2.

Summary

In this chapter we have discussed:

- The fact that Excel is a very powerful, yet easy to use, spreadsheet package.
- The minimum software and hardware requirements necessary to run the package successfully.
- The installation procedure for Excel.
- Accessing the package through the Start menu and the Shortcut Bar.
- The Excel screen.
- The difference between Workbooks and Worksheets.
- Utilizing the menu system using the mouse and the keyboard.
- The Office Assistant and On-line Help system.
- Exiting Excel.

02 basic excel skills

In this unit you will learn

- some spreadsheet jargon!
- about workbooks
- about entering and editing text, data and formulas
- about formatting cells
- how to move and copy data and formulas

Aims of this chapter

This chapter will introduce you to the basic skills you will need to work in Excel. By the time you have completed this chapter you will have created a simple worksheet and you will know how to create, edit, save, print, open and close a workbook.

2.1 Spreadsheet jargon

Before going any further, spend a little time getting familiar with some of the jargon you will encounter. There's nothing difficult about it – once you know what it means!

Rows, columns and cells

The worksheet area consists of rows, columns and cells. Rows are identified by the numbers down the left side of the worksheet area. Row 6 is highlighted in the illustration below. There are *lots* of rows on a worksheet – 65,536 in fact!

Columns are identified by letters displayed along the top of the worksheet area. Column C is highlighted in the illustration. After Z, columns are labelled AA to AZ, then BA to BZ, and so on to IV, giving 256 columns in all.

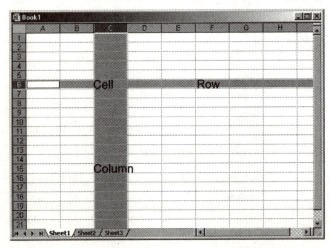

Where a row and column intersect you have a cell. Each of the rectangular areas on your worksheet is a cell. Cells are identified using a cell *name* or *address*. A cell address consists of the column letter followed by the row number of the column and row that intersect to create the cell.

Cell A1, B9, C3, D6 and F3 have been highlighted in the screenshot below.

Text, data, formulas and functions

The cells in your worksheet will eventually contain text, numeric data, formulas or functions.

Text is used for titles or narrative to describe the figures you are presenting – worksheet headings, column headings and row labels will usually be text entries.

Numeric data means the figures that appear in your worksheet. The data may be entered through the keyboard, or it may be generated as the result of a calculation.

Formulas are used to perform calculations on the numeric data in your worksheet (see section 2.10 and Chapter 5). Formulas are used to add the value in one cell to that in another or multiply the values in different cells, etc. Some of your formulas will be very basic while others may be quite complex.

Functions are predefined formulas that perform simple or complex calculations (see Chapters 5 and 6). There are many different kinds of functions set up in Excel – statistical, logical, financial, database, engineering – and many more. You're bound to find some useful ones, whatever type of data you work with.

2.2 File handling

In Excel, a file is called a workbook. Each new workbook you create is automatically given a temporary file name – *Book1*, *Book2*, etc. The name appears on the workbook Title bar.

There are several ways in which you can create new workbooks and open existing ones in Excel.

Task Pane

You can use the Task Pane that appears when you start Excel (if it doesn't display at startup you can show it by choosing **Task Pane** from the **View** menu).

- To create a new workbook from the Task Pane, choose **Blank Workbook**.

The workbooks that have been used most recently are listed at the top of the Task Pane, under **Open a workbook**.

- To open a workbook from the Task Pane, simply click on the one that you wish to open, or choose **More workbooks…** to display the **Open** dialog box.

New workbook

Whether or not the Task Pane is open, you can create a new blank workbook by clicking the **New** tool on the Standard toolbar.

Open a workbook

To open a workbook without the Task Pane:

1 Click the **Open** tool on the Standard toolbar

Or

- Open the **File** menu and choose **Open**.

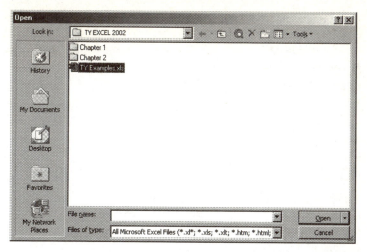

2. In the **Open** dialog box, locate and select the workbook
3. Click **Open**

If the workbook you want to open has been used recently, you may find it in the list of recently-used files in the **File** menu.

Save a workbook

At some stage you must save your workbook to disk (if you don't you will lose it when you switch off your computer). When you save your workbook, you should give it a file name that reflects its contents rather than use the *Bookx* temporary name.

To save your workbook:

1. Click the **Save** tool on the Standard toolbar
2. At the **Save As** dialog box, locate the folder in which you wish to save your workbook (usually *My Documents*)
3. Enter the name in the **File name:** field
4. Leave the **Save as type:** at *Microsoft Excel Workbook*
5. Click **Save**

You are returned to your workbook. The new name of the workbook appears on the workbook Title bar.

You can save your workbook at any time – you don't need to wait until you've entered all your data. I suggest you save your workbook regularly – and remember to resave it when you make changes to it. If you haven't saved your workbook, and your computer crashes or you have a power failure, you may lose any unsaved data.

Once a workbook has been saved, simply click the **Save** tool when you want to save any changes to it. If a workbook has already been saved, the Save As dialog box does not reappear, but the up-to-date version of your workbook replaces the old version already saved to disk.

Save As

There may be times that you save a workbook, edit it, then decide that you want to save the edited workbook but also keep the original version of the workbook on disk.

If you don't want to overwrite the old version of a workbook with the new edited version, save the new version using a different file name. You can save your workbook to the same folder if you want to, or you can select a different drive and/or folder.

1 Open the **File** menu and choose **Save As**.
2 The **Save As** dialog box will appear again. Enter a new name in the **File name:** field
3 Click **Save**

• If you save the new version of the file into the same folder as the old one, you must use a different file name.

Password protection

If you wish to password protect your workbook (so that no one can open or edit the workbook unless they know the password) you can do so from the **Save As** dialog box.

1 Click the **Tools** button on the **Save As** dialog box toolbar and choose **General Options**

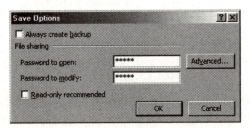

2. Enter the password(s)
3. Click **OK**
4. Re-enter the password(s) at the prompt
5. Click **OK**

Closing your workbook

To close your workbook:

- Open the **File** menu and choose **Close**.

Or

- Click the **Close** button in the top right of the window.

To work on a workbook that you have saved and closed, you must open it first.

2.3 Moving around your worksheet

Before you can enter anything into a cell, you must make the cell you want to work on *active*. To make a single cell active, you must select it. You can easily move onto any cell (thus making it active) using either the keyboard or the mouse.

The active cell has a dark border. The address of the active cell appears in the Name box to the left of the formula bar.

To make a cell active:

Using the mouse

* Click on the cell (you may need to use the horizontal or vertical scrollbars to bring the cell into view if it isn't on the screen).

Using the keyboard

* Use the right, left, up and down arrow keys to move right or left one column, or up or down one row at a time.
* Hold down [**Ctrl**] and press an arrow key to move to the last occupied cell in that direction.
* Press the [**Enter**] key to move onto the cell directly below the one that is currently active.

You can also go to a specific cell, if you know its address.

To go to a specific cell:

1 Press the [**F5**] key on your keyboard
2 Enter the address of the cell you want to go to in the **Reference** field of the **Go To** dialog box
3 Click **OK**

To return to cell A1 from anywhere in your worksheet:

* Hold down the [Ctrl] key and press [**Home**].

To move to the end of the work area on your worksheet (the last cell you have worked on, rather than cell IV65536):

* Hold down the [Ctrl] key and press [**End**].

Check out *Keyboard shortcuts* in the on-line Help to see if there are any others that you would find useful.

2.4 Selection techniques

You will often work on more than one cell at a time in Excel. You may need to format a group of cells in a particular way or copy or move a group, or apply a function to a group.

A group of cells is called a cell range. Cell ranges are identified by the first cell address in the range, then a colon, followed by the last cell address, e.g. A1:A7, C3:D12, F5:H7. These ranges are highlighted in the picture below.

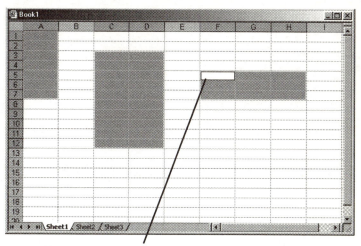

Note that the first cell selected is not highlighted

Using the mouse

To select a group of adjacent cells:

1 Click and drag over the range of cells you wish to select

Or

1 Click on a cell in one corner of the range you wish to select
2 Hold the [**Shift**] key down on your keyboard
3 Click on the cell in the diagonally opposite corner of the range you want to select

To select a row or rows:

• Click the row number to the left of the row you want to select.

Or

• Drag down over the row numbers to select several rows.

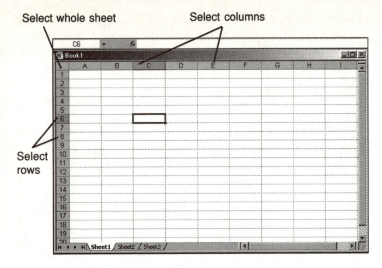

To select a column or columns:

- Click the letter at the top of the column you want to select.

Or

- Drag across the column letters to select several columns.

To select the whole worksheet:

- Click the box at the top of the row numbers, and left of the column letters.

To select a range of non-adjacent cells:

1 Click on one of the cells you want to select
2 Hold the [**Ctrl**] key down
3 Click on each of the other cells you want to select

To deselect a range of cells:

- Click on any cell outside the range.

Using the keyboard

To select a group of adjacent cells:

1 Click in a cell that will be in the corner of the range you wish to select
2 Hold the [**Shift**] key down

3 Press the arrow keys to move to the cell in the corner diagonally opposite, and release the [**Shift**] key

To deselect a range of cells:

- Press one of the arrow keys.

2.5 Entering text and numeric data

Each time you start Excel a new workbook is created. To use this new workbook, close the Task Pane (if necessary) and enter your data. Entering text or data into your worksheet is easy.

1 Select the cell you want to enter text or data into
2 Type in the text or data – the text or data will appear in the formula bar as well as in the active cell
3 Press [**Enter**] or click the 'tick' button to the left of the formula bar when you've completed the cell

Things to note when entering numeric data:

- If you have adjusted the width of a column (see section 2.7) then enter data that is too large for the width, the cell will display ######## signs instead of the figures. When this happens you must either change the number format (see section 2.9) or adjust the width again (see section 2.7).
- Numbers align by default to the right (see section 3.2).

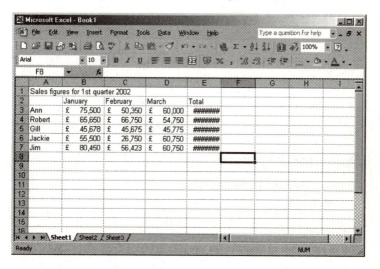

Things to note when entering text:

- Text that doesn't fit into a single cell will 'spill over' into the cell to the right if that one is empty.
- Text that doesn't fit into a single cell will be only partially displayed if the cell to the right is not empty. You will need to widen the column (see section 2.7) to display all of the text.
- Text aligns by default to the left of a cell (see section 3.2).

2.6 Editing text and numeric data

If you make an error when entering data, you can fix things by:

- Deleting the contents of the cell.
- Replacing the contents of the cell.
- Editing the contents or the cell.

To delete the contents of a cell (or cells):

1 Select the cell (or cells) whose contents you want to erase
2 Press the [**Delete**] key on your keyboard

To replace all the contents of a cell:

1 Select the cell whose contents you want to replace
2 Type in the text or data that should be in the cell

To edit the contents of a cell:

1 Select the cell whose contents you want to edit
2 Click in the Formula bar
3 Edit the cell contents as required (you can move right and left using the arrow keys, delete characters using the [**Delete**] or [**Backspace**] key, or enter text or data through the keyboard)
4 Press [**Enter**] on your keyboard when you've finished editing to return to the sheet

Or

1 Double-click in the cell whose contents you want to edit – this places the insertion point within the cell
2 Edit the cell contents as required
3 Press [**Enter**] on your keyboard when you've finished editing

Examples in this book

Throughout this book we will use several different worksheets to illustrate various features in Excel. I suggest you enter these examples into a workbook and use them as practice material. You can then follow the instructions in the book and experiment with the features.

Simon's Sports

The first worksheet will display a list of items that are in a sale in Simon's Sports. We will use this worksheet to demonstrate some of Excel's features as you work through the rest of this chapter. Enter the text displayed in the worksheet below and build up the worksheet as you work through the rest of the chapter.

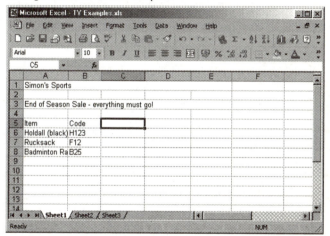

2.7 Column width

If the text you are entering into a cell is more than the column width will accommodate, you must do something about it if you want it to be fully visible.

Sometimes – particularly with main headings at the top of a worksheet – it doesn't matter if the text spills over into the cells to the right. However, when entering column headings or row labels each entry should occupy a single cell – with no over-spill into the next column.

One way to make text fit into a single cell is to adjust the column width.

Manual adjustment

To change the width of a column:

- In the column heading row, click and drag the vertical line to the right of the column whose width you want to change – in this example we need to widen column A.

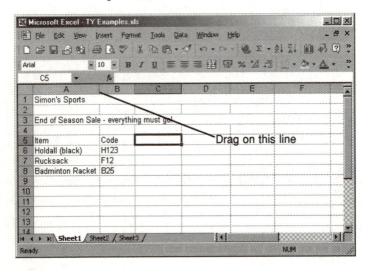

AutoFit

You can get Excel to automatically adjust the width of the column to fit the entries within it.

To adjust the column width automatically:

- In the column heading row, double-click the vertical line to the right of the column you want to adjust.

Format menu

You can also adjust the column width from the Format menu.

To set a specific column width using the Format menu:

1 Select any cell in the column you want to adjust
2 Open the **Format** menu and choose **Column**
3 Choose **Width**

4 Complete the **Column Width** dialog box – the value is the number of characters that can be displayed in the standard font.

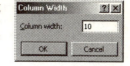

5 Click **OK**

To automatically adjust the column width from the Format menu:
1 Select the cell that will determine the column width required for your column
2 Open the **Format** menu and choose **Column**
3 Click **AutoFit Selection**

To change the default column width for your columns:
1 Open the **Format** menu and choose **Column**
2 Choose **Standard Width**
3 Set the size in the **Standard Width** dialog box
4 Click **OK**

2.8 Text wrap within a cell

Sometimes it is best to force a text entry to *wrap* within a cell, rather than have to widen a column to accommodate it. This applies particularly to headings. Consequently it may be useful to set the *Text wrap within cell* option for the row that contains your column headings.

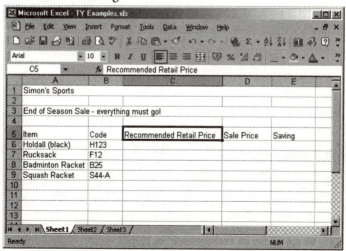

In the last example, monetary values will eventually go in the *Recommended Retail Price* column and will only take up 6 or 7 characters. To widen the column to accommodate 'Recommended Retail Price' would result in a rather strange looking layout in our final worksheet.

To specify that text should wrap within a row of cells:

1 Select the row you want to set the text wrap option for
2 Open the **Format** menu and choose **Cells...**
3 Select the **Alignment** tab
4 Select the **Wrap text** checkbox
5 Click **OK**

Experiment with other options to see what effect they have

Column heading with **Wrap text** turned on

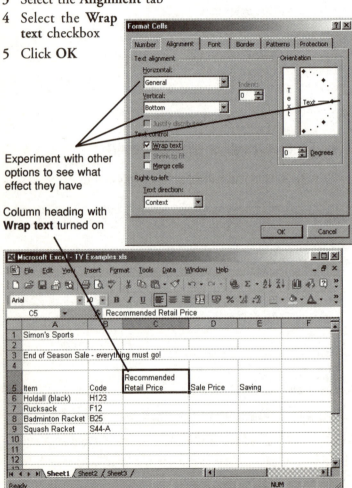

Adjust the column widths as necessary to get the effect you want.

- If the row height does not adjust automatically to accommodate the text when it wraps, choose **Row** from the **Format** menu, then select **AutoFit**.

Shrink to fit

If the contents of a cell are just *too* wide for the column width, and you don't want to widen the column, you can get the contents of the cell to 'shrink to fit'.

1. Select the cell whose contents you want to shrink to fit
2. Open the **Format** menu and choose **Cells...**
3. On the **Alignment** tab, select the **Shrink to fit** checkbox and click **OK**

2.9 Number formats

A lot of the data entered into a worksheet is currency. Most of the times that you enter currency values, you will want the appropriate currency symbol to precede the figure – usually, but not always, the £ symbol.

If you want the £ symbol in front of a figure you can either:

- Format the cells to display the entry in a currency format.

Or

- Enter the £ symbol through the keyboard.

If you enter your figures through the numeric keypad, it's probably easiest to format the cells to display the figures as currency.

You can format cells *before* or *after* you have entered your text or data.

To format the cells to display the figures in currency format:

1. Select the cells you want to format (see section 2.4 above)
2. Click the **Currency** tool on the **Formatting** toolbar

The **Formatting** toolbar has other tools to help you format numbers – Percent Style, Comma Style, Increase and Decrease

	A	B	C	D	E
1	Simon's Sports				
2					
3	End of Season Sale - everything must go!				
4					
5	Item	Code	Recommended Retail Price	Sale Price	Saving
6	Holdall (black)	H123	£ 15.50	£ 9.99	
7	Rucksack	F12	£ 16.99	£ 9.99	
8	Badminton Racket	B25	£ 24.00	£ 15.99	
9	Squash Racket	S44-A	£ 27.75	£ 19.99	

Decimal (these two change the number of decimal places displayed). Other number formats can be found in the **Format Cells** dialog box, on the **Number** tab – have a look to see if any would be useful to you. The Euro is in the Currency category.

To apply a format from the Format Cells dialog box:

1. Select the cells you want to format
2. Open the **Format** menu and choose **Cells...**
3. Select the **Number** tab
4. Choose a category from the list
5. Complete the dialog box as required – exactly what appears in it depends on the category you select
6. Click **OK**

- **To enter the € symbol** through the keyboard, your number lock should be on, then press [Alt] - 0128. (Check out the on-line Help for more information on Euros.)

2.10 Formulas

Any cell in your workbook, which will contain a figure that has been calculated using other entries in your workbook, should have a formula or function in it (do *not* do your calculations on a calculator, then type the answer in to your workbook).

Formulas allow you to add, subtract, multiply, divide and work out percentages of the values in cells.

Operators used in formulas are:

+	Add	–	Subtract
/	Divide	*	Multiply
%	Percentage		

In our example we are going to use a formula to work out how much a customer will save if they buy something out of the sale.

To work out the saving for the first item in the list (the holdall), we need to subtract the sale price (the figure in cell D6) from the recommended retail price (the figure in cell C6). The result of this calculation should be displayed in cell E6, in the Saving column.

To enter the formula required:

1 Select the cell that will contain the result of the calculation (E6 in this example)
2 Press the [=] key on your keyboard (to tell Excel we're entering a formula)
3 Click on cell C6 (the recommended retail price cell for the item)
• The cell address appears in the formula bar *and* in the current cell.
4 Press the [–] key on your keyboard (we're subtracting)

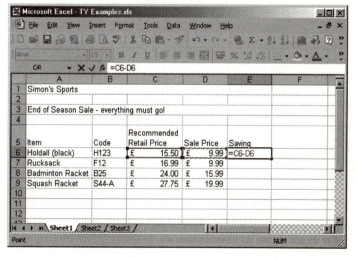

5 Click on cell D6 (the cell containing the *sale price* figure)
6 Press [**Enter**] on your keyboard
* The result of the calculation will appear in cell E6.

At step 3 and step 5 above, I suggested you click on the cell you want to use in your formula. If you prefer, you can enter the cell address manually by typing the coordinates into your formula instead.

Simple formula examples

=A7/B6   Divide the figure in A7 by the figure in B6

=D22*12 Multiply the figure in D22 by 12

=C7*25% Calculate 25% of the figure in C7

Order of precedence

If there is a mixture of operators in a formula, Excel will deal with the multiplication and division *before* it deals with the addition and subtraction.

=A4+C7*D7   Multiply the figure in C7 by the one in D7, and add the answer to the figure in A4

=A1+B2/C3+D4*E5-F2 Add to the figure in A1, the result of dividing the figure in B2 by that in C3, then add the result of multiplying the figure in D4 by that in E5, then subtract the figure in F2 (phew!!)

Parentheses

Some formulas can become quite long and complicated – and tricky to follow! If you want to force the order in which a formula is worked out, or even just make a long formula easier to read, you must use parentheses ( ).

In the example below, the problem within each set of parentheses is solved *before* working through the formula.

=(A1+B2)/C3+(D4*(E5-F2))

Add A1 to B2	we'll call this XX
Subtract F2 from E5	we'll call this YY
Multiply YY by D4	we'll call this ZZ

To get the final result:

Divide XX by C3 then add ZZ

I hope you followed that!

To help you remember this, think BODMAS! Brackets over Division and Multiplication, then Addition and Subtraction. *Always* work left to right and *never* move the position of the entries you are calculating.

2.11 AutoFill

In Simon's Sports sale worksheet, we could work down the column entering the formula for each *Saving* cell as described in section 2.10 above. However, a much quicker way to achieve the same result is to use the AutoFill option.

AutoFill allows you to *copy* a formula from one cell into adjacent cells – to the right, left, up or down.

To AutoFill the formula in E6 to the other cells in the Saving column:

1 Select E6
2 Position the pointer over the bottom right corner of the cell – the Fill Handle (a small black cross) should appear
3 Click and drag the black cross down over the other *Saving* cells

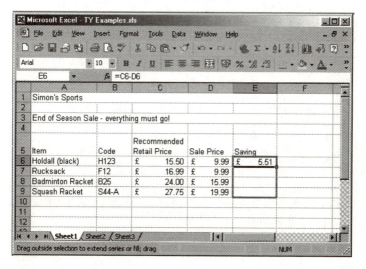

When you release the mouse, the formula in cell E6 will be copied to the cells you dragged over.

If you click on each cell in the saving column and keep an eye on the Formula bar, you will notice that Excel has automatically changed the cell addresses in the formula *relative* to the position you have copied the formula to. Neat trick!

When you AutoFill text or data, a Smart tag appears below the data that you have copied. Click the Smart tag to see the AutoFill options. If you don't want the default, click the option required.

AutoFill can be a real time-saver in some situations. Try the following:

If you need to enter column or row labels for each month of the year or day of the week:

1 Enter the first month or day you want to use into the appropriate cell – January or Jan, September or Sept, Wednesday or Wed
2 AutoFill the contents of that cell across the columns or down the rows
• Excel will automatically complete the other cells.

If you need to enter a row or column of numbers in sequence, e.g. 1, 2, 3, 4 etc. or 50, 100, 150 etc.:

1 Enter the first two numbers in two adjacent cells
2 Select both cells
3 AutoFill down the rows or across the columns

If you want to enter dates, you can use the Fill option. The date can be incremented using every day of the week (day), weekdays only (Monday to Friday), months or years.

1 Enter the first date in your series
2 Click and drag the **Fill Handle** using the *right* mouse button
3 When you release, a pop-up menu appears
4 Select the fill option you require – **Fill Days**, **Fill Weekdays**, **Fill Months** or **Fill Years**

	A	B	C	D	E	F	G
1					Step value 10	Fill Years	Fill Weekdays
2	Jan	January	Monday	MON	10	01/01/2000	04/12/2000
3	Feb	February	Tuesday	TUE	20	01/01/2001	05/12/2000
4	Mar	March	Wednesday	WED	30	01/01/2002	06/12/2000
5	Apr	April	Thursday	THU	40	01/01/2003	07/12/2000
6	May	May	Friday	FRI	50	01/01/2004	08/12/2000
7	Jun	June	Saturday	SAT	60	01/01/2005	11/12/2000
8	Jul	July	Sunday	SUN	70	01/01/2006	12/12/2000
9	Aug	August	Monday	MON	80	01/01/2007	13/12/2000
10	Sep	September	Tuesday	TUE	90	01/01/2008	14/12/2000
11	Oct	October	Wednesday	WED	100	01/01/2009	15/12/2000
12	Nov	November	Thursday	THU	110	01/01/2010	18/12/2000
13	Dec	December	Friday	FRI	120	01/01/2011	19/12/2000

Examples of some of the Fill options are displayed above.

- Column A and B show different month formats AutoFilled.
- Column C and D show different day formats AutoFilled.
- Column E shows figures with an increment of 10 AutoFilled.
- Column F has been completed using the Fill Years option on the pop-up menu.
- Column G has been completed using the Fill Weekdays option on the pop-up menu.

2.12 Another worksheet!

Use this example to get some more practice. Enter the text and data below into a different worksheet in your workbook. To select a different worksheet, click the sheet tab – Sheet1, Sheet2, Sheet 3, etc. to the left of the horizontal scroll bar. It doesn't matter what sheet you use. This example is for a stock value table for *Screw the Nut plc*. Use the following notes to help you get the layout and formulas correct.

- Enter the main headings, and column headings, *Part No*, *Description*, *Cost (trade)*, *Cost (retail)*, *Profit* and *Number in Stock*.
- Format row 5 to allow text wrap within the cells (see section 2.8).
- Format the data cells in the *Cost (trade)*, *Cost (retail)*, *Profit*

and *Value of Stock* columns to display the figures as currency (see section 2.9).

- Enter a formula to calculate the *Profit* figure. For the first item (screwdriver set) it would be **=D6-C6** (see section 2.10 for information on entering formulas).
- The *Number in Stock* figures are centred in this example (see section 3.2).
- Enter a formula to calculate the *Value of Stock* column. For the first item it would be **=C6*F6** (if you base the stock value on the trade price).
- AutoFill the formulas down the columns (see section 2.11).
- The *Total value of Stock* figure could be calculated by entering the formula **=G6+G7+G8+G9** (you could also use the AutoSum function for this – see section 5.1).

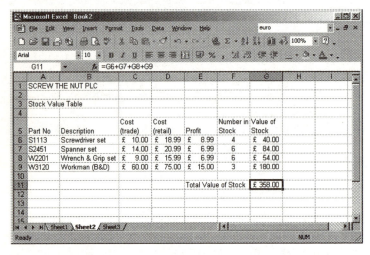

2.13 Move or copy cell contents

If you enter text or data into your worksheet, and it's the right text or data, but in the wrong place you can move it to where it should be (rather than delete it and re-type it in the correct location).

To move the contents of cells:

1 Select the cells you want to move

2. Click the **Cut** tool ✂ on the Standard toolbar
3. Select the top leftmost cell of the range you want to move the text or data to
4. Click the **Paste** tool 📋 on the Standard toolbar

Or

1. Select the cells you want to move
2. Point to the edge of the selected area – the mouse pointer displays four directional arrows
3. Drag and drop the selected cells into the correct position

To copy the contents of cells:

1. Select the cells you want to copy
2. Click the **Copy** tool 📋 on the Standard toolbar
- A dotted line appears around the cells to be copied.
3. Select the top leftmost cell of the range you want to copy the text or data to
4. Click the **Paste** tool 📋 on the Standard toolbar
- If you want more than one copy, repeat steps 3 and 4 until you have all the copies required.
- Click the **Paste** Smart tag to display the copy options.
5. Press [**Esc**] to cancel the dotted line around the copied cells

Or

1. Select the cells you want to copy
2. Point to the edge of the selected area – the mouse pointer displays four directional arrows
3. Hold down the [**Control**] key (the mouse pointer changes to a white pointer shape with + beside it) while you drag and drop the selected cells. (Make sure you release the mouse button *before* the [**Control**] key – if you don't, you'll end up moving the cells instead of copying them).

Paste Special

There may be times when you wish to copy and paste in Excel, but you want to be selective about what you paste – the functions, formatting, comments etc. Or you might want to paste data and add, subtract, multiply or divide it into existing data. You can use Paste Special when this is the case.

1 Copy or cut the data
2 Select the cell(s) that you want to paste the data into
3 Open the **Edit** menu
4 Choose **Paste Special**
5 Select the items you wish to paste e.g. **Values**
6 Choose the operation you want performed with the pasted data (if any)
7 Click **OK**

2.14 Insert and delete rows and columns

As you build up your worksheet, you may discover that you have added a row or column that you don't require, or perhaps missed out a row or column that you do need.

To insert a row:

1 Select the row (see 2.4) that will go *below* the row you are inserting
2 Right-click within the selected area and choose **Insert** from the pop-up menu

To insert a column:

1 Select the column (see 2.4) that will go to the right of the column you are inserting
2 Right-click within the selected area and choose **Insert**

To delete a row or column:

1 Select the row or column (see 2.4) you wish to delete
2 Right-click within the selected area and choose **Delete**

To add or delete several rows or columns at the same time:

1 Click and drag in the row or column label area to indicate how many rows or columns you want to insert or delete
2 Right-click within the selected area and choose **Insert** or **Delete** as required

2.15 Print preview and print

At some stage you will want to print your file. Before printing, it's a good idea to *preview* it. It takes practice to get a good fit, and you may find it useful to plan things in rough before you begin to draw up your worksheet. Page layout options are discussed in section 3.9.

Print Preview

To preview your worksheet:

- Click the **Print Preview** tool on the Standard toolbar.

A preview of the current worksheet will be displayed on your screen, in full-page view. It doesn't matter if you can't read what is on the screen – the preview is there to let you see how your worksheet will fit onto your paper. You get an idea of how well the data, white space, graphics, etc. will look on the page.

If you want to change something when you see the preview:

1 Click the **Close** tool on the Print Preview toolbar to return to your worksheet

2 Edit the worksheet as required
3 Preview again to see how it looks

Print

When you are happy with the preview, you can send it to print.

If you are in Print Preview:

1 Click **Print...** on the Print Preview toolbar
2 Complete the **Print** dialog box – set **Number of copies** and **Print range** as required
3 Click **OK**

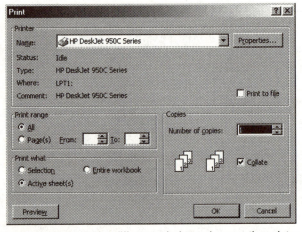

Your Print dialog box may be different – it depends upon the printer

If you have your worksheet displayed (not in Print Preview):

- Click the **Print** tool on the Standard toolbar.

One copy of the current worksheet will be sent to your printer.

Print part of your worksheet

If you don't want to print all of your worksheet, you can print the area required on its own. To print part of your worksheet:

1 Select the range of cells you want to print
2 Open the **File** menu and choose **Print...**
3 Select **Selection** from the **Print what** options
4 Click **OK**

Summary

In this chapter we have discussed some of the basic skills required when using Excel. We have discussed:

- Spreadsheet jargon.
- Cell names and ranges.
- File handling – Save, Close, Open and New.
- Moving around a worksheet.
- Selection techniques – for rows, columns, adjacent and non-adjacent cells.
- Entering text and numeric data.
- Deleting, replacing and editing the contents of a cell.
- Adjusting column widths.
- Wrapping text within a cell and 'shrink to fit'.
- Number formats.
- Entering simple formulas.
- Order of precedence and the use of parentheses.
- AutoFill.
- Moving and copying cells.
- Inserting and deleting rows and columns.
- Print Preview and Print.

03 formatting and layout

In this unit you will learn

- some more formatting options
- how to freeze panes
- how to split the screen
- how to set page layout options

> **Aims of this chapter**
>
> In this chapter we will consider some of the cell formatting options that you can use to improve the presentation of a worksheet. We will also discuss ways of viewing different areas of a worksheet on the screen at the same time. Finally, to help you get your printouts exactly as you want them, we'll look at some of the page layout options.

3.1 Bold, italic and underline

You can make the contents of a cell (or cells) bold, italic or underlined using either the Formatting toolbar or keyboard shortcuts.

Formatting toolbar

1. Select the cells you wish to make bold, italic or underline
2. Click the **Bold** [B], the *Italic* [I] and/or the Underline [U] tool on the Formatting toolbar
3. Deselect the cells

The bold, italics and underline tools are toggles – they are used to switch the formatting on or off.

To remove bold, italics or underline formatting from a cell or cells:

1. Select the cell(s) you wish to remove the formatting from
2. Click the Bold, Italic and/or Underline tool
3. Deselect the cells

Keyboard shortcuts

1. Select the cell or cells you wish to format
2. Apply or remove the formatting with these keyboard shortcuts
- **[Ctrl]-[B]** for bold
- **[Ctrl]-[I]** for italics
- **[Ctrl]-[U]** for underline
3. Deselect the cells

3.2 Alignment

When entering text and data into your worksheet, the default alignment of text is to the left, the default of numeric data is to the right. You can change the alignment of text or data within a cell if you wish, either before or after you enter your text or data.

Left, right and centre

1 Select the cells required
2 Click the **Align Left** tool on the Formatting toolbar to align the cell contents to the left

Or

- Click the **Center** tool to align to the centre.

Or

- Click the **Align Right** tool to align to the right.

Centre across selection

If you want to merge cells and centre the data in a cell across them, you can use the Merge and Centre tool. This is useful when you want to centre a heading across several columns in your worksheet – perhaps the text in the title row.

Item	Code	Rec Retail Price	Sale Price	Saving
Holdall (black)	H123	£ 15.50	£ 9.99	£ 5.51
Rucksack	F12	£ 16.99	£ 9.99	£ 7.00
Badminton Racket	B25	£ 24.00	£ 15.99	£ 8.01
Squash Racket	S44-A	£ 27.75	£ 19.99	£ 7.76

Simon's Sports — End of Season Sale - everything must go!

To centre text or data across several columns:

1 Select the range of cells you want to centre the text or data across, e.g. A3:E3
2 Click the **Merge and Centre** tool

3.3 More formatting options

The default font used in Excel worksheets is Arial, the default font size is 10. You can change the font used or the font size if you wish.

The colours of the text and background can be set as required, and you can add borders to any or all sides of a block of cells if you want to make them really stand out.

To change the font:

1 Select the cells
2 Click the drop-down arrow to the right of the **Font** field on the Formatting toolbar
3 Choose an alternative font from the list (use the scroll bar if necessary to bring the font required into view)

To change the font size:

1 Select the cells you want to modify
2 Click the drop-down arrow to the right of the **Font Size** field on the Formatting toolbar
3 Choose an alternative font size from the list (use the scroll bar as necessary)

To change the font colour:

1 Select the cell (or cells)
2 Click the drop-down arrow to the right of the **Font Color** tool on the Formatting toolbar
3 Click on the colour you want to use

To change the background colour of a cell:

1. Select the cell (or cells)
2. Click the drop-down arrow to the right of the **Fill Color** tool
3. Click on the colour you want to use

To apply a border to a cell (or cells):

1. Select the cell (or cells)
2. Click the drop-down arrow by the **Border** tool
3. Select the border effect you wish to use
4. Deselect your cell (or cells)

Draw Border

If you choose **Draw Border** from the **Borders** options, the **Borders** toolbar appears and the mouse pointer becomes a pencil.

You can use this pencil to *draw* the borders in that you require.

To create your border:

1. Choose the **Line Style** and **Line Color** required using the tools on the toolbar
2. Click on the grid line where you want your border to appear (or drag along it if you want the border to cross a number of rows or columns)
- You can also create diagonal lines within a cell be dragging from one corner to the one diagonally opposite.

To erase a border:

1. Click the **Erase Border** tool
2. Click (or drag along) the border you want to remove

Format Cells dialog box

The formatting options can also be found in the Format Cells dialog box, on the Alignment, Font, Border and Patterns tabs.

To display the dialog box:

- Choose **Cells...** from the **Format** menu.

Experiment with the formatting options in your worksheets.

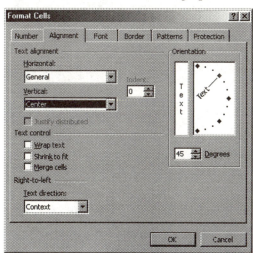

Angled text is useful for headings in narrow columns

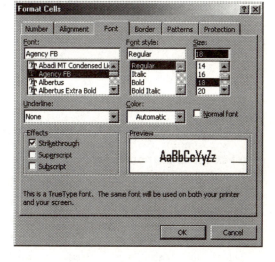

There are more Font effects – and a preview – on the Font tab

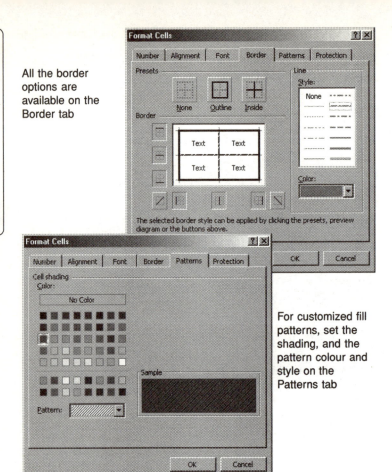

All the border options are available on the Border tab

For customized fill patterns, set the shading, and the pattern colour and style on the Patterns tab

3.4 Format Painter

If you have applied several formatting options to a cell, and you want to apply the same formatting to some other cells in your worksheet you could save yourself some time by using the Format Painter.

The Format Painter allows you to copy the formatting from one cell, and paint it on to other cells.

To copy a format to a single cell, or to adjacent cells:

1 Select the cell that is formatted the way you want

2. Click the **Format Painter** tool on the Standard toolbar
3. Click on the cell you want to apply the formatting to

Or

- Click and drag over the cells that you want to apply the formatting to.

To copy a format to non-adjacent cells:

1. Select the cell that is formatted the way you want
2. Double-click the **Format Painter** tool on the Standard toolbar – this 'locks' the Format Painter tool on
3. Click on each cell you want to apply the formatting to

Or

1. Drag over the cells you want to paint with the formatting.
2. Click the Format Painter tool again (or press [**Esc**]) to switch the Format Painter off when you've finished

3.5 Conditional formatting

Conditional formatting is used to format a cell (or range of cells), if specific conditions are met.

You may have a list of figures, and decide that you want all those that are >=50000 displayed in red and italics, and all those figures that are <50000 displayed in green.

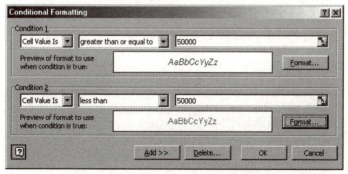

1. Select the cells that you want to apply the formatting to
2. Open the **Format** menu and choose **Conditional Formatting...**

3 Set the **Condition 1** criterion

4 Click the **Format...** button and set the formatting required

5 Click **Add>>** so that you can specify another criteria (if required – you can specify up to 3 conditions)

6 Complete the dialog box as required

7 Click **OK**

3.6 Change the default font

If you don't want to use the default font of Arial, size 10, you can change it. *Once you have changed the default font, you must restart Excel before it will take effect.* Every new workbook you create will use the font you have specified as the default (until you change it again).

To change the default font:

1 Open the **Tools** menu and choose **Options**

2 Select the **General** tab

3 Set the **Standard font:** and **Size:** fields as required

4 Click **OK**

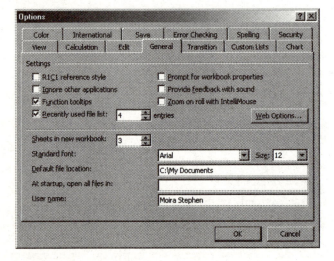

5 Click **OK** at the prompt that appears

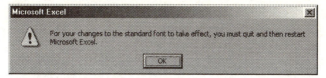

6 Exit Excel and restart it again for the change to take effect

3.7 Freeze panes

Many of the worksheets you create will be considerably larger than will fit on to your computer screen. You will need to scroll vertically and horizontally to display the data you want to work with.

When you scroll your worksheet, the column headings or row labels will disappear off your screen as the other data appears. This is often inconvenient, as you need to see the headings and labels to make sense of your data. In these situations you should *freeze* the heading columns and rows so that they stay in place and only the data cells scroll.

To freeze a row (or rows):

1 Select the row below the ones you want to freeze

Or

To freeze a column (or columns):

• Select the column to the right of the ones you want to freeze.

Or

To freeze both a row (or rows) and column (or columns):

• Select the cell below and to the right of where you want to freeze the panes.

2 Open the **Window** menu
3 Choose **Freeze Panes**

The worksheet will be divided into separate panes.

When you scroll through your worksheet horizontally, the column or columns you have frozen remain in view. When you scroll through your worksheet vertically the row or rows you have frozen will remain in view when the other data scrolls.

The heavy line indicates the edge of the frozen pane
Rows 1–4 are frozen

	A	B	C	D	E	F
1		Simon's Sports				
2		End of Season Sale - everything must go!				
3						
4	Item	Code	Rec Retail Price	Sale Price	Saving	
8	Squash Racket	S44-A	£ 27.75	£ 19.99	£ 7.76	
9	Hockey Stick	H220	£ 16.99	£ 9.99	£ 7.00	
10	Hockey Stick	H221	£ 18.99	£ 10.99	£ 8.00	
11	Tennis Racket	T101	£ 35.99	£ 24.99	£ 11.00	
12	Badminton Racket	B17	£ 18.99	£ 14.00	£ 4.99	
13	Rucksack	R10	£ 14.99	£ 9.99	£ 5.00	
14	Dumbell Set	D12	£ 36.99	£ 26.99	£ 10.00	
15	Home Gym	HG3	£ 245.99	£ 175.00	£ 70.99	

To unfreeze panes:

1 Open the **Window** menu
2 Choose **Unfreeze Panes**

3.8 Split screen

There will also be times when you want to compare the data on one part of your worksheet with that on another – but the data ranges that you want to compare are in separate areas of the worksheet. When this happens, you should *split* your screen so that you can scroll each part independently, to bring the data you require into view.

Split box

If you look carefully at the top of the vertical scroll bar (above the up arrow), or to the right of the horizontal scroll bar (outside the right arrow), you will notice the *split box*. Use these to split your screen.

To split your screen horizontally:

- Drag the split box at the top of the vertical scroll bar down to where you want your split to be.

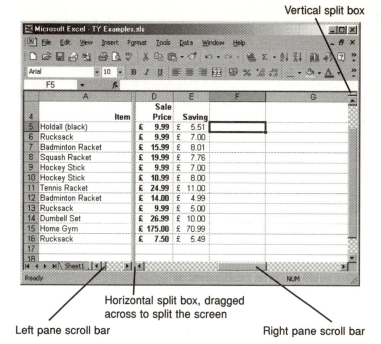

Vertical split box

Horizontal split box, dragged across to split the screen

Left pane scroll bar

Right pane scroll bar

To split your screen vertically:

- Drag the split box at the right of the horizontal scroll bar along to where you want your split to be.

When your screen is split, you can scroll each pane independently to view the data you want to see.

To remove a split:

- Double-click the split.

3.9 Page layout

In Chapter 2 we discussed printing. We will now consider some ways in which you can change the appearance (or layout) of the printed sheet.

Orientation

Pages are usually printed portrait (rather than landscape) on A4 paper.

To change the orientation:

1 In a worksheet, open the **File** menu and choose **Page Setup**

Or

- In Print Preview, click the **Setup…** button on the Print Preview toolbar to open the Page Setup dialog box.

2 Select the **Page** tab
3 Choose the orientation option – *portrait* or *landscape*
4 Click **OK**

Scaling

If your worksheet is more than a page in size, you can specify the number of pages you want it to be printed on using the **Scaling** option.

1 Open the **Page Setup** dialog box and select the **Page** tab
2 In the **Scaling** options, specify the number of pages wide and tall you want your worksheet to fit on
3 Click **OK**

- This option is particularly useful if the last page of your worksheet contains only a small amount of data. You can specify that the worksheet print on one page less than it really needs – Excel will scale the worksheet down to fit onto that number of pages.

Page size

The default paper size used for printing is A4. You can select an alternative page size.

1 Open the **Page Setup** dialog box and select the **Page** tab
2 Choose the size required for the **Paper size** list
3 Click **OK**

Margins

You can change the margin settings for a worksheet in either Page Setup or in Print Preview.

To change the margins in the Page Setup dialog box:

1 Open the **Page Setup** dialog box and select the **Margins** tab
2 Specify the margins you want to use
3 Click **OK**

To change the margins while in Print Preview:

1 Click the **Margins** button on the Print Preview toolbar
* The margins appear as dotted lines around your page.
2 Drag the margins to the position required

Page breaks

If a worksheet runs to more than one page, Excel will divide it into pages by inserting automatic page breaks. Exactly where the page breaks appear depends on the paper size, margin settings and scaling options you have set. You can set your own horizontal and vertical page breaks.

To insert a horizontal page break:

1 Select the row *below* where you want the page break to be
2 Open the **Insert** menu and click **Page Break**

To insert a vertical page break:

1 Select the column to the *right* of where you want to insert the page break
2 Open the **Insert** menu and click **Page Break**

To insert a horizontal and vertical page break at the same time:

1 Select the cell immediately below and to the right of where you want to start a new page
2 Open the **Insert** menu and click **Page Break**

To move a page break:

1 Open the **View** menu and click **Page Break Preview**
* The first time you go into Page Break Preview a prompt appears to tell you how to move the breaks – if you don't want this prompt to appear again, select the checkbox and click **OK**.
2 Drag the page break to its new position

To remove a page break:

1 Open the **View** menu and click **Page Break Preview**
2 Right-click on a cell below a horizontal page break

Or

- Right-click on a cell to the right of the vertical page break.
3 Click **Remove Page Break** on the shortcut menu
4 Open the **View** menu and click **Normal** to return to your worksheet

Headers and footers

Headers and footers display information at the top or bottom of every page that prints out for your worksheet. They are useful for page numbers, your name, the date that the worksheet is printed, the worksheet name, the workbook name – or any other information that you would like to appear in them.

To add a header and/or footer to your pages:

1 Open the **Page Setup** dialog box
2 Select the **Header/Footer** tab
3 Choose a header or footer from the list of options
4 Click **OK**

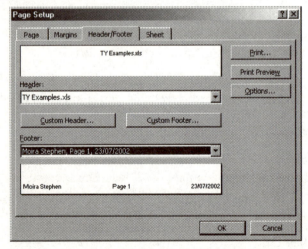

You don't need to use one of the options listed. You can set up any header or footer you want.

To set a custom Header or Footer:

1. Select the **Header/Footer** tab in the **Page Setup** dialog box
2. Click **Custom Header…** or **Custom Footer…**
3. Click in the section you want your header or footer to appear in – left, centre or right
4. Type in the text you want to appear in the header or footer

Or

- Click the appropriate button to add page numbers, date, time, folder, file or sheet name, or a picture, or to use the Format Painter.

5. Click **OK**

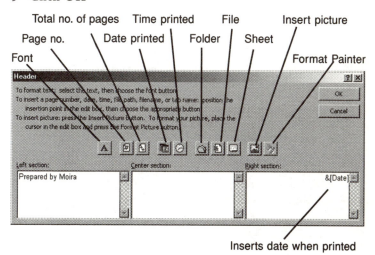

Gridlines, row and column headings

When you print your worksheet out, the gridlines, row and column headings do not print. This is usually how you would want it, but there may be times when it is useful to print out the gridlines and/or the row and column headings – for example, when printing out the formulas and functions you have used (see Chapter 5).

You can specify that you want the gridlines, row and column headings to print in the **Page Setup** dialog box.

1. Open the **File** menu and choose **Page Setup**, then select the **Sheet** tab
2. In the Print options, select the **Gridlines** and/or **Row and column headings** checkboxes as required
3. Click OK

Page order

If your worksheet is going to print out on more than one sheet of paper, the pages can be printed **down then over** OR **over then down**. You can specify the order you prefer.

1. Open the **Page Setup** dialog box and select the **Sheet** tab
2. In the **Page order** options, select the order required
3. Click OK

Summary

This chapter has discussed some of the options available to help you format your worksheet. We've also looked at how you can freeze and split your screen and how you can modify the layout of a worksheet before you print it. We have considered:

- Bold, italic and underline.
- Alignment options – left, right, centre, merge and centre.
- Font, font size, font colour, background colour, cell borders in individual cells or ranges on the worksheet.
- The Format Painter.
- Changing the default font.
- Keeping column headings and row labels displayed by freezing panes.
- Viewing different parts of a worksheet on the screen at the same time by splitting the screen.
- Page layout options – orientation, scaling, page size, margins, page breaks, headers and footers, gridlines, row and column headings and page order.

04

working with sheets

In this unit you will learn
- about worksheet layout
- how to insert, delete and rename worksheets
- about moving and copying worksheets
- how to group worksheets

> **Aims of this chapter**
>
> This chapter addresses some of the options you will find useful when working with worksheets. We will discuss some things you might like to consider when designing a worksheet. You will learn how to add worksheets to a workbook, delete, rename, copy and move them. You will also find out how to group worksheets and enter data, text or formulas on several worksheets simultaneously.

4.1 Moving between worksheets

The worksheet tabs appear at the bottom left of your screen – to the left of the horizontal scrollbar.

To move from one sheet to another in your workbook:

- Click the sheet tab of the sheet you want to work on.

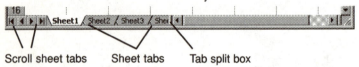

Scroll sheet tabs   Sheet tabs   Tab split box

If you can't see all the sheet tabs in the sheet tab bar, you can use the buttons to the left of the sheet tabs to scroll the sheet tabs into view.

You can change the amount of space allocated to the sheet tab bar and the horizontal scroll bar by dragging the Tab split box between the sheet tabs and the horizontal scroll bar.

4.2 Worksheet design

Before you start setting up a worksheet, you should give some thought to its design. The main areas to keep in mind are:

- Work out the purpose of your worksheet. Ask yourself:
  - What do you want to communicate?
  - What should be emphasized or de-emphasized?
  - How will you show the relationship between areas?

- Keep it simple.
- Be consistent – within a worksheet and across worksheets. If you produce the same worksheet every month, regular readers will be able to find the information they need quickly if it's always in the same place.
- Use formatting and layout options to add contrast to different areas of your worksheet.

There are no hard and fast rules – the main objective is to display the data in a clear and unambiguous way. If you like your worksheet layout and your audience can understand it, it's probably okay.

Some Dos and Don'ts of worksheet design

DO make sure you use a font that is easy to read – Arial (the default) is a very 'clean' font, Times New Roman is easy on the eye.

DO make use of 'white space' – leave some blank rows or columns between sections of your worksheet to make it easier to read.

DO use borders and/or shading effects to divide large worksheets up into manageable chunks and to draw attention to subtotals and totals.

DO format your numbers appropriately – currency, number of decimal places, percentage, etc.

DO make sure your worksheet is legible – don't use too small a font size or shrink to fit data to the extent it is too small to read.

DO add comments to cells that need an explanation.

DON'T use too many different fonts or font sizes on a worksheet.

DON'T overdo font and fill colours – you'll give readers a headache!

DON'T print gridlines out on a final report – they will give it a very cluttered look, though they may be useful on a draft printout, or one with formulas displayed.

4.3 Inserting worksheets

When you create a workbook in Excel the default number of worksheets is three. This may be enough (or more than enough), but if you need more than three in a workbook you can easily add them.

To insert a worksheet:

1 Select a worksheet (click on the sheet tab)
2 Open the **Insert** menu and choose **Worksheet**

Or

1 Right-click on a tab
2 Choose **Insert** from the shortcut menu
3 Select the **General** tab in the **Insert** dialog box

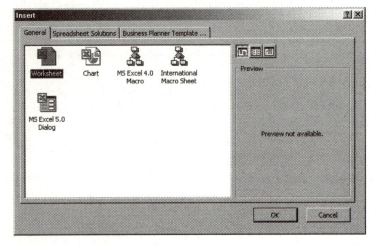

4 Choose **Worksheet** and click **OK**.
* The worksheet will be inserted to the left of the selected one, but can be moved as required (see section 4.6).

Default sheets in a workbook

If you need to add new worksheets to most of your workbooks, you could change the default number of sheets in a new workbook to save you always having to add more.

To change the default number of sheets in a workbook:

1 Open the **Tools** menu and choose **Options**
2 Select the **General** tab
3 Set the number of sheets you require in the **Sheets in new workbook:** field
4 Click **OK**

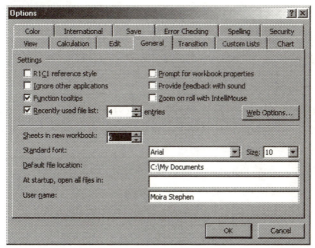

4.4 Deleting worksheets

If a workbook has too many sheets you can delete any you don't need.

To delete a worksheet:

1 Select the sheet you want to delete
2 Open the **Edit** menu and choose **Delete Sheet**

Or

1 Right-click on the sheet tab of the sheet you want to delete
2 Select **Delete** from the shortcut menu
3 Respond to the prompt – click **Delete** if you really want to delete the sheet, **Cancel** if you change your mind

Be careful when deleting worksheets – **Undo** will not restore them!

4.5 Renaming worksheets

By default, worksheets are named *Sheet1*, *Sheet2*, etc. If you only use one or two sheets in a workbook this may cause you no problems. However, if you have several worksheets, life would be a bit easier if you renamed them with a name that actually meant something.

To rename a worksheet:

1 Select the worksheet you want to rename
2 Open the **Format** menu, choose **Sheet**, then **Rename**
3 The sheet tab name will become selected – type in the name you want to use
4 Press [**Enter**] or click anywhere on the worksheet

Or

1 Double-click on the sheet tab you want to rename
2 Type in the name you want to use
3 Press [**Enter**] or click anywhere on the worksheet

4.6 Moving and copying worksheets

If you want to change the position of a worksheet within your workbook, you can move it to the position required. You can also move a worksheet to a new workbook or to another open workbook.

To move a worksheet:

1 Select the worksheet you want to move or copy
2 Open the **Edit** menu and choose **Move or Copy Sheet...**
3 Choose the book you want to move or copy the worksheet to in the **To book:** field
4 Select a sheet – this doesn't apply if you choose *New book* in the **To Book:** field

5 Select **Create a copy** if you want to make a copy of the sheet rather than move it

6 Click **OK** – the sheet will be inserted before the one you selected

♦ If you move or copy your worksheet to a new book, remember to save the new workbook if you want to keep it.

You can also move or copy worksheets within a workbook by dragging the worksheet tab to the position required.

To move the worksheet:

♦ Click and drag the worksheet tab of the sheet you want to move along the sheet tabs until it is in the correct place.

To copy the worksheet:

♦ Click on the worksheet tab, hold the [**Ctrl**] key down and drag the worksheet tab to the required position.

4.7 Grouping worksheets

There may be times when you want to enter the same text, data or formulas into corresponding cells in more than one worksheet.

You could enter your work onto one worksheet, then copy it onto the others, or, you could group the worksheets together and enter the standard text, data, formula and/or functions that will appear on them all.

When worksheets are grouped, anything you do on one worksheet is automatically entered onto every worksheet in the group.

To group adjacent worksheets:

1 Click on the sheet tab of the first sheet you want in the group

2 Hold the [**Shift**] key down and click on the last sheet tab you want in the group

To group non-adjacent worksheets:

1 Click on the sheet tab of the first sheet in the group

2 Hold the [**Ctrl**] key down and click on each sheet tab that you want in the group

When worksheets are grouped the word [**Group**] appears on the workbook Title bar.

To ungroup worksheets:

1 Click on any worksheet tab that isn't part of the group

Or

1 Right-click on one of the grouped worksheet tabs

2 Choose **Ungroup Sheets** from the pop-up menu

Summary

In this chapter we have discussed:

- Moving between sheets in a workbook.
- Things to consider when designing a worksheet layout.
- Inserting sheets into a workbook.
- Changing the default number of sheets in a workbook.
- Deleting sheets from a workbook.
- Renaming sheets.
- Moving and copying sheets within a workbook.
- Moving and copying sheets to a new workbook.
- Grouping worksheets.

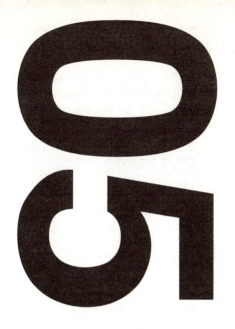

05 formulas and functions

In this unit you will learn

- more about functions and formulas
- about relative and absolute addresses and circular references
- how to use named ranges
- how to add comments and protect your worksheet

Aims of this chapter

This chapter continues our discussions of formulas (introduced in Chapter 2) and introduces some of the many Excel functions that you might find useful. We will discuss AutoSum, statistical functions, named ranges, cell comments and worksheet protection.

5.1 AutoSum

The worksheet below contains details of quarterly sales figures. Enter the text and data into a new worksheet in your workbook. We need to calculate the total sales figures for each sales representative for the year and also the total sales figure for each quarter.

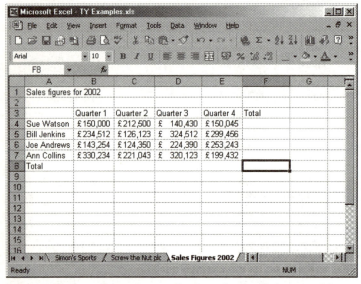

You could use a formula to calculate the total (e.g. in F4 you might have **=B4+C4+D4+E4**), but the easist and quickest way to calculate it is with AutoSum.

To calculate the totals using AutoSum:

1 Select a cell in which you want a total figure to appear, e.g.

the cell that will contain the total sales for the first sales person or the total for Quarter 1

2 Click the **AutoSum** tool Σ on the Standard toolbar
3 The range of cells to be added together will be highlighted. Note that the function also appears in the formula bar.
4 If the suggested range of cells is correct, press [**Enter**]

Or

- If the suggested range is *not* the range of cells you want to add, drag over the correct range, then press [**Enter**].

The total value of the selected range will appear in the active cell when you accept the formula by pressing [**Enter**].

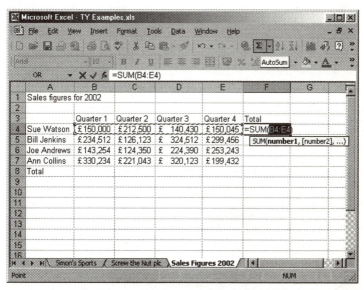

- Excel calculates the total value of the selected cells using the SUM function. Its syntax is =**SUM** (**cell range**) – you could type in the function, but it's usually easier (and less error prone) to use AutoSum.

You could select each of the total cells in turn and use AutoSum to calculate the values that should appear in them, or use AutoFill (see section 2.11) to copy the function down or across the other total cells.

If you are totalling rows and columns as in this example, you could use a shortcut that performs all the calculations in one move.

To AutoSum several groups of cells simultaneously:

1 Select all of the rows and columns to total, and the cells to contain the results of the AutoSum calculations

2 Click the **AutoSum** tool on the Standard toolbar

The cells in the rightmost column and bottom row of the selected area will each have the Sum function inserted into them.

Non-adjacent cells

You can also use AutoSum to total non-adjacent cells if you wish.

To total non-adjacent cells:

1 Select the cell that will contain the result of the calculation
2 Click the **AutoSum** tool on the Standard toolbar
3 Click on the first cell you want to include in the range of cells
4 Hold the [**Ctrl**] key down and click on each of the other cells to be included in the function
5 Press [**Enter**]

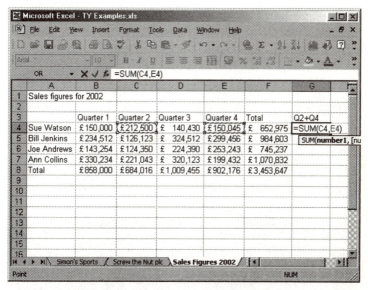

- If you prefer to type in the function, you must start with = (equals sign). A range of adjacent cells has the first cell address in the range entered, followed by : (colon), then the last cell address in the range. The cell addresses for non-adjacent cells must be separated by , (comma).

5.2 Inserting a function

Excel has many functions that you can use on your data. There are statistical, financial, logical, text, database, lookup, data and time functions, etc. It is very unlikely that you will need to use them all (you'll be glad to know), but we'll look at some of the functions that are useful at a general level. You can then go on and explore the functions and find any that may be useful in your particular situation. Use the online Help as necessary.

To insert a function:

1 Select the cell that you want the function to go in
2 Click the function button *fx* (to the left of the formula bar)
• The **Insert Function** dialog box is displayed

Search for a function:

1 Enter details of what you want to do in the **Search for a function** field
2 Click **Go**
• Excel will display a list of functions that it thinks might help in the 'Recommended' category
3 Scroll through the list to see what's there
4 Select the function and click **OK**

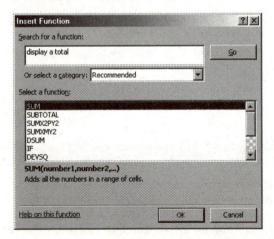

Selecting a function (without searching):

1 Select the category that your function is in (choose **All** if you're not sure which category)
2 Scroll through the list until you find the function you need
3 Select it and click **OK**
* You can get help on any function from this dialog box if you select it and click **Help on this function**.

Once you've selected a function the **Function Arguments** dialog box appears.

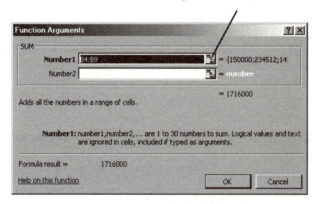

Minimize the dialog box to adjust or change the selected cells

* If the **Function Arguments** dialog box obscures the area of the worksheet you want to view, click the 🔲 button to the right of a data entry field – it will become minimized, so you can see your worksheet.
* To display the dialog box again, click the restore button at the far right of the minimized window.

Restore

5.3 Statistical functions

These include MIN, MAX, AVERAGE and COUNT, which can be used to display a value from a range of cells.

MIN   returns the smallest value
MAX   returns the largest value
AVERAGE   returns the mean average value (= total / count)
COUNT   returns the number of numeric entries
COUNTA   returns the number of numeric and text entries

Return to your Simon's Sports worksheet (probably *Sheet 1*). Under the list of items for sale, enter functions to display:

* The **minimum** figure from the *Saving* column
* The **maximum** figure from the *Saving* column
* The **number** of items in the sale
* The **average** sale price of the items in the list

Work through the first of these (minimum) following the instructions, then try the others yourself.

1 Select the cell that the minimum value will be displayed in
2 Click the **Insert Function** button
3 Choose the **Statistical** category
4 Select **MIN**
5 Click **OK**

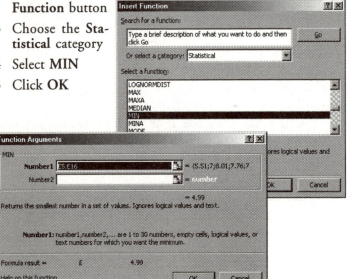

6 Enter the range of cells that you want the function to operate over in the Number1 field – either drag over the range on the worksheet, or type in the cell addresses (minimize the dialog box so you can see the worksheet if necessary)

7 Restore the dialog box if necessary

8 Click **OK**

To edit a function:

1 Select the cell that contains the function

2 Edit the function in the formula bar

Or

• Click the **Insert Function** button again to display the **Function Arguments** dialog box

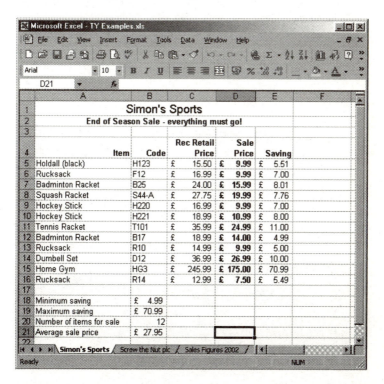

5.4 View formulas

When setting up your worksheet, it is sometimes useful to display and print the formulas and functions that you have entered into the cells.

Each formula or function is displayed in the formula bar when its cell is selected, but you can get Excel to display all the formulas and functions in your worksheet if you wish.

To display the formulas and functions:

1 Open the **Tools** menu and choose **Options…**
2 Select the **View** tab
3 Select the **Formulas** checkbox and click **OK**

* The keyboard shortcut [**Ctrl**] – [|] (above the [**Tab**] key) toggles the display of formulas.

You may need to adjust the column widths to display the whole formula or function in some columns.

* You can print a copy of your worksheet out with the formulas and functions displayed – a printout is often useful for reference purposes.

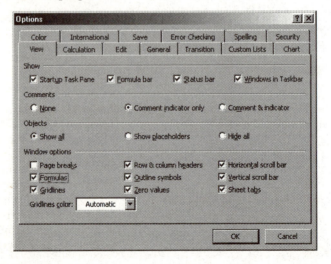

The formulas and functions used in the Simon's Sports worksheet are displayed opposite – note that what you can see is the data exactly as it was entered, and not as it is displayed on screen.

Simon's Sports

End of Season Sale - everything must go

Item	Code	Rec Retail Price	Sale Price	Saving
Holdall (blue)	H123	15.5	9.99	=C6-D6
Rucksack	R12	16.99	9.99	=C7-D7
Badminton Racket	B25	24	15.99	=C8-D8
Squash Racket	S44-A	27.75	19.99	=C9-D9
Hockey Stick	H220	16.99	9.99	=C10-D10
Hockey Stick	H221	18.99	10.99	=C11-D11
Tennis Racket	T101	35.99	24.99	=C12-D12
Badminton Racket	B17	18.99	14	=C13-D13
Rucksack	R10	14.99	9.99	=C14-D14
Dumbell Set	D12	36.99	26.99	=C15-D15
Home Gym	HG3	245.99	175	=C16-D16
Rucksack	R14	12.99	7.5	=C17-D17

Minumum Saving	=MIN(E6:E17)
Maximum Saving	=MAX(E6:E17)
Number of items in sale	=COUNT(E6:E17)
Average sale price	=AVERAGE(D6:D17)

The **Formula Auditing** toolbar appears when your formulas are displayed. You can use this toolbar to identify which cells are dependent on others, and which cell values have precedents.

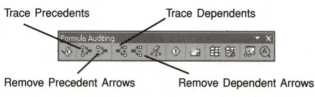

Trace Precedents — Trace Dependents
Remove Precedent Arrows — Remove Dependent Arrows

Experiment with the Trace/Remove Precedents and Dependents arrows on the toolbar to see which cells are influenced by, or have an influence on, the values in other cells.

If you select cell E10 then click the **Trace Precedents** and **Trace Dependents** tools, arrows will appear showing the relationship of E10 to other cells in the worksheet (see next page). We can see that the value in cell E10 is dependent on the values in C10 and D10, and that those in B18, B19 and B20 are influenced by the value in E10. This graphical representation of the relationship between cells can be useful when you need to check what is going on in a worksheet. You can remove the arrows selectively using the **Remove Precedent Arrows** and **Remove Dependent Arrows** as required, or click **Remove All Arrows**.

* To hide the formulas and functions again, go back to the **View** tab in the **Options** dialog box, deselect the **Formulas** checkbox and click **OK**.

	B	C	D	E
1	Simon's Sports			
2	of Season Sale - everything must go!			
3				
4	Code	Rec Retail Price	Sale Price	Saving
5	H123	15.5	9.99	=C5-D5
6	F12	16.99	9.99	=C6-D6
7	B25	24	15.99	=C7-D7
8	S44-A	27.75	19.99	=C8-D8
9	H220	16.99	9.99	=C9-D9
10	H221	18.99	10.99	=C10-D10
11	T101	35.99	24.99	=C11-D11
12	B17	18.99	14	=C12-D12
13	R10	14.99	9.99	=C13-D13
14	D12	36.99	26.99	=C14-D14
15	HG3	245.99	175	=C15-D15
16	R14	12.99	7.5	=C16-D16
17				
18	=MIN(E5:E16)			
19	=MAX(E5:E16)			
20	=COUNT(E5:E16)			
21	=AVERAGE(D5:D16)			

5.5 Relative and absolute addresses

You have already noticed that when you AutoFill or copy a formula or function, the cell addresses used in the formula or function change automatically, relative to the position you copy them to.

By default, the cell addresses used are *relative addresses*.

There will be times when you use a cell address in a formula, and want to copy the formula down some rows or across some columns, but don't want the cell address to change relative to its new position.

In the next example, we are going to calculate the income from admissions to a film centre.

- Enter the data onto a new worksheet in your workbook (see section 4.3 if you need to add a new sheet). DO NOT complete the Revenue columns – we will enter formulas to calculate the figures in these columns.

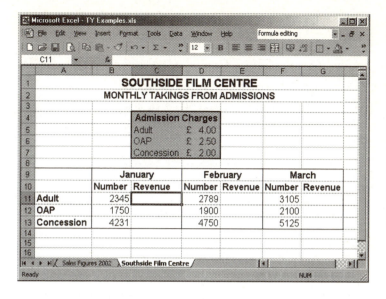

To calculate the January revenue figures:

1 Enter a formula into the *Adult* cell in the *January, Revenue* column to calculate the income from this group. The first revenue figure for January is calculated by multiplying the number of adults (B11) by the adult admission rate (D5). The formula in C11 should be =B11*D5.

2 Use AutoFill (see section 2.11) to copy the formula down over the *OAP* and *Concession* cells

We could enter the appropriate formulas into the February and March columns in a similar way. However, it would be quicker to *copy* the January formulas. This poses two possible problems:

* We **don't** want the D5 (adult rate), D6 (OAP rate), D7 (concession rate) cell addresses to change when we copy the formula across.

* We can't use AutoFill because the cells we want to copy to are not next to the source cells.

To stop the cell addresses from changing when we copy them, we must create *absolute addresses* for them. An absolute address will not change when the formula or function containing it is copied or moved.

To create an absolute cell address:

- Enter a $ sign in front of each coordinate you want to fix.

You can type the $ sign, or use the [**F4**] key on your keyboard.

To absolutely address the cells in a formula:

1 Select the cell that contains the formula (C11, C12 or C13 in this example) – the formula appears in the Formula bar

2 Click in the Formula bar

```
= =B11*$D$5
```

3 Place the insertion point to the *right* of the cell address you want to make absolute (D5 or D6 or D7)

4 Press [**F4**] until you have the cell addressed properly

- Each time you press [**F4**] it moves through the absolute addressing options.

D5	neither coordinate will change
D$5	the column will change if you copy the formula across columns
$D5	the row number will change if you copy the formula down rows
D5	both coordinates will change relative to its new position

Absolutely address the admission rate cell address in each of the January formula – either D5 or $D5 will do. We will later copy the formula across the columns, but must look back to column D for our data.

Once you've made the appropriate cell addresses absolute, you can copy the formula across to the February and March columns.

To complete the February and March figures:

1 Select the cells you are copying from – the *January* revenue figures in this case, C11:C13

2 Click the **Copy** tool on the Standard toolbar

3 Select the first cell you want to paste into e.g. E11 for the *February* figures – you don't need to select E11:E13

Whitby Public Library (Dundas Branch)
29 APR 2003 11:31am
Patron id: 142343

Excel 2002 /
39342500047932   Due: 20 MAY 2003 +

Microsoft Excel 2000 simplified /
39342499205101   Due: 20 MAY 2003 +

DUNDAS BRANCH HOURS:
Monday through Friday
9:30 a.m. to 9:00 p.m.
Sat. 9:00 a.m. to 5:00 p.m.

****

Items may be renewed once
using ARNIE and overdue items renewed on
ARNIE are subject to fines.
Call ARNIE at: 905.430.7913.

****

****

4 Click the **Paste** tool on the Standard toolbar
5 Select cell G11 as the first cell for the *March* figures
6 Click the **Paste** tool on the Standard toolbar
7 Press [**Esc**] on your keyboard to cancel the copy routine

Your final worksheet should look similar to the one below. The first picture displays the formulas (you may have different cell addresses if you have used different rows and columns for your data), the second one shows the results.

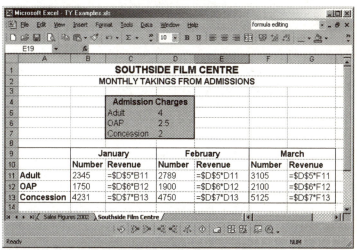

5.6 Circular references

If you create a formula that refers to its own cell, you have a *circular reference*. Excel cannot resolve these using normal calculation methods and a warning will appear should one occur.

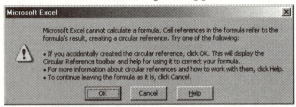

Read the Help page that appears, and minimize it so that you can refer back to it quickly if necessary.

* The Circular Reference toolbar has **Trace Precedents**, **Trace Dependents** and **Remove All Arrows** tools (similar to the Formula Auditing toolbar – see 5.4) so that you can display the arrows to help you work out what is going on.

To review and amend circular references:

1 Go to the first cell that is registering a circular reference – use the **Navigate Circular Reference** box on the toolbar
2 Study the formula or function – if you spot the error, amend as necessary

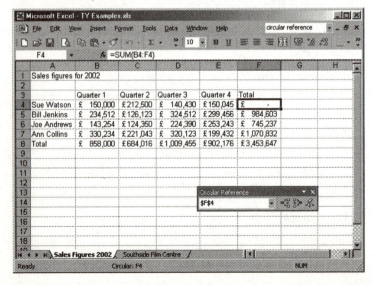

3 If you can't see what is wrong, try the next cell that is causing a problem (click the drop-down arrow on the **Navigate Circular Reference** box)

4 Review and edit the cells as necessary, until you have solved the problem

- When the circular reference problem is resolved, the Circular Reference toolbar will disappear.

- Note that the status bar says 'Circular', with the address of the cell that is causing the problem, when a circular reference is present. This will disappear when you have solved the problem. If no cell address is present, the *active* worksheet does not contain the circular reference.

Some engineering and scientific formulas require circular references – in this case you may need to change the number of iterations (the number of times Excel recalculates the sheet).

To change the number of iterations:

1 Choose **Options** from the **Tools** menu

2 On the **Calculation** tab, select the **Iteration** checkbox then specify the maximum number of iterations and degree of change you want Excel to use.

5.7 Named ranges

When building up your formulas and functions, you have been using cell addresses to tell Excel which cells you want to use in your calculations. Cell addresses are not really very user-friendly – it isn't always immediately clear what the formula =**B13*B6** or the function =**AVERAGE(D5:D17)** is actually doing.

To make your worksheet easier to understand you can use *named ranges* instead of cell addresses in your formulas and functions.

There are two main ways of naming ranges.

You can either:

- Use the existing labels that are on your worksheet to refer to the related data.

Or

- Create new descriptive names.

Create named ranges

You can easily give a cell or range of cells a name. The name used can be anything you like (as long as it obeys the rules below) or you can use column and/or row labels as names for your cell ranges. Named ranges that you create are available to any worksheet within the workbook.

Rules for naming ranges:

- The maximum size for a name is 255 characters.
- Spaces are not allowed (use an underline or a full stop).
- The first character in a name *must* be a letter or an underline character (other characters can be letters, numbers, full stops and underlines, but not commas, question marks or other punctuation characters).
- You *cannot* use a cell reference for a range name, e.g. B75 or AA$24.
- Names can contain upper and lower case letters. Excel is *not* case sensitive. If you create a name called *Profit*, then another called *PROFIT*, the second will replace the first.

To name a cell, or range of cells, within a worksheet:

1. Select the cell or range of cells you want to name
2. Click the **Name** box at the left edge of the formula bar

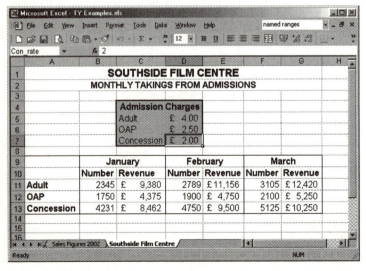

3 Type in a name for the cells
4 Press [**Enter**]

You could name the ranges for the admission charges in the Film Centre worksheet, with names such as *Adult_rate*, *OAP_rate* and *Con_rate*.

To name cells using the existing row and column headings:

1 Select the cells you want to name – including the row and/or column headings
2 Open the **Insert** menu and choose **Name**, then **Create**
3 In the **Create Names** dialog box, select the location that contains the labels by ticking the appropriate checkbox(es)
4 Click **OK**

You could create named ranges for the columns in the *Screw the Nut plc* worksheet using this method.

You can easily paste range names into your formula or function, rather than using the cell addresses.

To use a range name in a formula or function:

1 Select the cell that will contain your formula
2 Enter the formula as normal *until* you want to refer to a named range
3 Open the **Insert** menu, choose **Name** then **Paste**
4 Select the name you want to paste, then click **OK**
5 Continue writing the formula

If you no longer use a range name, you can delete it. Deleting the range name *does not* delete the cell contents, but it will affect any cells that refer to the named range in a formula.

To delete a range name:

1 Open the **Insert** menu and choose **Name**, then **Define**
2 Select the range name you want to delete
3 Click **Delete** and close the **Define Name** dialog box

Converting cell addresses to named ranges

If you find that you prefer using named ranges to cell addresses in your worksheets, but you have already created formulas using cell addresses, you can easily convert these cell addresses to named ranges for all or part of your worksheet. Create names for the ranges of cells that you want to convert – see above.

1 To convert all of the cell addresses in your formulas to named ranges, select any single cell in your worksheet

Or

To convert only part of your worksheet, select the range of cells required:

2 Open the **Insert** menu, choose **Name** then **Apply**
3 Select the names you want to apply from the **Apply names list**
4 Click **OK**

• If you have created named ranges for the columns in the Screw the Nut plc worksheet, try converting the formulas using this method.

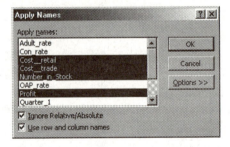

• The cell addresses in the formulas will have been replaced by the range names.

The Screw the Nut plc worksheet is displayed opposite, top. The cell addresses originally used in the formulas were converted to the named ranges using the method described above.

```
                    SCREW THE NUT PLC
                     Stock Value Table

Part                    Cost   Cost                              Number
No    Description      (trade) (retail)  Profit                 in Stock  Value of Stock
S1113 Screwdriver set    10    18.99   =Cost__retail-Cost__trade    4     =Cost__trade*Number_in_Stock
S2451 Spanner set        14    20.99   =Cost__retail-Cost__trade    6     =Cost__trade*Number_in_Stock
W2201 Wrench & Grip set   9    15.99   =Cost__retail-Cost__trade    6     =Cost__trade*Number_in_Stock
W3120 Workman (B&D)      60    75      =Cost__retail-Cost__trade    3     =Cost__trade*Number_in_Stock

                                       Total value of stock              =SUM(Value_of_Stock)
```

5.8 Comments

If you think that the purpose of a formula or function in a cell is not self-explicit, you can add a *comment* to the cell. You will find comments particularly useful if you don't use named ranges, and want to add an explanation to a cell, or, if others share your worksheets and you want to explain the logic behind an entry you have made.

To add a comment to a cell:

1   Select the cell you want to add a comment to
2   Hold down the [**Shift**] key and press [**F2**]

Or

◆   Open the **Insert** menu and choose **Comment**.

3   Type your comment into the box
4   Click outside the comment box

If the comment remains on your screen, I suggest you change the comment view options to show the comment indicator only.

1   Open the **Tools** menu and choose **Options**
2   Select the **View** tab
3   In the **Comments** options, select the **Comment indicator only** radio button

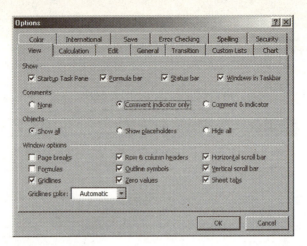

A small red triangle will appear in the top right corner of your cell to indicate it has a comment attached to it.

When you move your mouse pointer over the cell, the comment will be displayed.

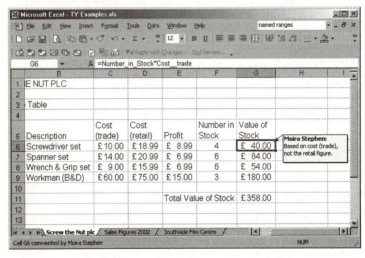

To edit a comment:

1 Select the cell that has the comment attached to it
2 Right-click on the cell and select **Edit Comment** from the shortcut menu that appears

Or

* Hold down the [**Shift**] key and press [**F2**].
3 Edit the comment as required
4 Click outside the comment box

To delete a comment:

1 Select the cell that has the comment attached to it
2 Right-click on the cell and select **Delete Comment** from the shortcut menu that appears

The Reviewing toolbar can be used to help you create, edit and delete comments. To display the toolbar, choose **Toolbars** from the **View** menu and select **Reviewing** from the list.

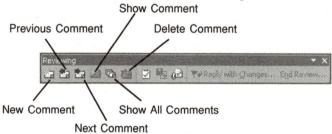

5.9 Worksheet protection

Having gone to the trouble of setting up formulas and functions on your worksheet, it would be a pity if they were accidentally overwritten when you are entering text and data. You can protect your worksheet to avoid this unfortunate situation arising.

When you protect a worksheet, cells formatted as *locked* cannot be edited, cells formatted as *unlocked* can. Initially **all** cells are locked. You must therefore unlock cells that you want to be able to edit in the protected sheet, before you turn on protection.

Once the worksheet has been protected, only those cells that you unlocked can be modified (unless you 'unprotect' the worksheet again).

To identify the cells that are not to be locked:

1 Select the cells
2 Open the **Format** menu and choose **Cells...**

3 Select the **Protection** tab
4 Deselect the **Locked** checkbox
5 Click **OK**

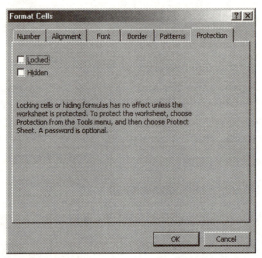

To activate the protection:

1 On the **Tools** menu, point to **Protection** and select **Protect Sheet...** or **Workbook...**
2 Tick the elements to be protected
3 Set a password if you wish – just don't forget it!
4 Click **OK**

To deactivate the protection:

1 Open the **Tools** menu, point to **Protection** and select **Unprotect Sheet...** (or whatever option is appropriate)
2 If you used a password, you'll be asked to enter it. Enter the password and click **OK**.

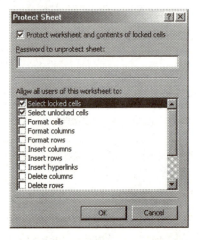

Summary

This chapter has concentrated on features that are particularly useful when working with formulas and functions. We have discussed:

- AutoSum.
- Inserting a function from the Formula Palette.
- The Statistical functions MIN, MAX, AVERAGE, COUNT and COUNTA.
- Viewing the formulas and functions in your worksheet.
- Relative and absolute cell addresses.
- Circular references.
- Named ranges.
- Adding comments to a cell.
- Worksheet protection.

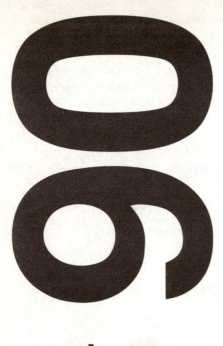

06 more functions

In this unit you will learn

- about Logical, Statistical, Math, Text, Date and Financial functions
- how to use Lookup tables
- about Data Tables, Scenarios and PivotTables

Aims of this chapter

In this chapter we will look at a number of functions from the different categories. Some logical, statistical, math, text, date, financial and lookup functions will be explored. Database functions will be considered in Chapter 9. We will also look at Data Tables, Scenarios and Pivot Tables.

6.1 Logical functions

IF function

The IF function is used to return one value if the condition you specify is True, and another value if the condition is False. The values returned can be text, numbers, or the result of a formula or function.

For example, you might be entering student end-of-term exam results into your worksheet. If a student has 50% or more in the exam, a pass will be awarded, if less than 50% is achieved, the result is a fail.

	A	B	C	D
1	END OF TERM EXAM RESULTS			
2				
3	Firstname	Surname	Total Mark	Result
4	Gill	McLaren	57	
5	Peter	Shaw	63	
6	Kim	Stephen	79	
7	Andrew	Borthwick	75	
8	Alison	Peterson	66	
9	Amanda	Mitchell	76	
10	Gordon	Williamson	38	
11	Clare	Stephen	83	
12	Jack	Williamson	77	
13	Ann	Shaw	42	

Comparison operators

This example uses a comparison operator to check if the Total Mark is greater than or equal to 50. The operators include:

=	equal to	<>	not equal to
>	greater than	>=	greater than or equal to
<	less than	<=	less than or equal to

Enter the data on the previous page into a new worksheet:

- To return a Pass or Fail message in the Result column, we need to enter the IF function.

You can use either cell addresses or named ranges in the function.

To enter the function:

1 Select the first cell in the result column

2 Click the **Insert Function** button f_x to the left of the formula bar

3 Select IF from the function list – you'll find it in the **Logical** category

4 Enter the condition that you want to be evaluated in the **Logical test** field *(Total_Mark>=50 in this case)*

5 Specify the value if the condition is found to be True – you don't need to type in the quotes – Excel will enter them automatically as it builds the formula.

6 Specify the value if the condition is found to be False

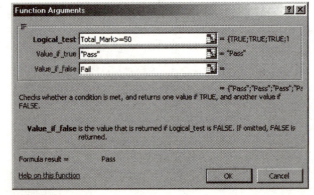

7 Click **OK**

- AutoFill the function down through the Result column – Pass will appear in the rows where the condition is true, Fail will appear in the rows where the condition is false.

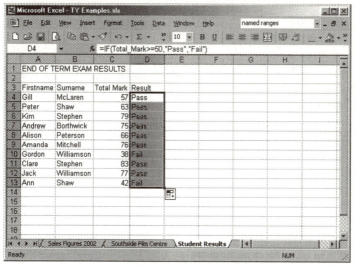

With the formulas displayed, the worksheet looks like the illustration below. This example uses named ranges rather than cell addresses. If we had used cell addresses the function would have been =IF(C4>=50, "PASS", "FAIL"), etc.

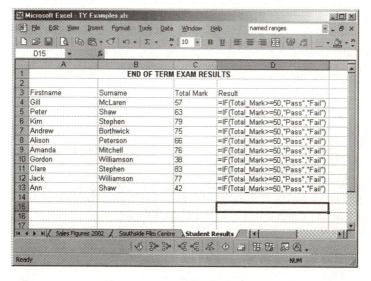

Nested IFs

The values used by functions to perform calculations or operations are called arguments. An argument may be a numeric value, a text value, a cell reference, a range of cells, a named range, or a nested function (a function within a function).

This next example illustrates nested IFs. We are going to add another column to our worksheet to give the Grade achieved by each student. We need to use the IF function to check the Total Mark and return the appropriate grade.

- IF a student gets 70% or more the grade is an A.
- IF the student gets 60% to 69% the grade is a B.
- IF the student gets 50% to 59% the grade is a C.
- Less than 50% is a fail.

As we have four possible outcomes this time (rather than a simple Pass or Fail) we must nest our IF functions to work through the various options.

- Add a new column heading, 'Grade', in the column to the right of the *Result* column.

1 Select the first cell in the *Grade* column

2 Click the **Insert Function** button *fx* and select IF from the function list

3 Enter the condition that you want to be evaluated in the **Logical test** field (*Total_Mark>=70* in this case) and specify the **Value if true** – A (70% and over gets an A)

4 In the **Value if false** field, select IF again (from function list to left of formula bar) – we need to check if a student has 60% or more. (This test will only be applied to students who *did not* get 70% or more.)

5 Complete the next set of conditions and values. Enter the condition that you want to be evaluated in the **Logical test** field (*Total_Mark>=60* in this case) and specify the **Value if true** – B (60% to 69% gets a B grade).

6 In the **Value if false** field select the IF function again – we need to check if the student has 50% or more (this test will only be applied to students who *did not* get 60 – 69%)

7 Enter the **Logical test** field data (*Total_Mark>=50* in this case)

8 Specify the **Value if true** – C (50% – 59% gets a C grade) and the **Value if false** – Fail
9 Click **OK**

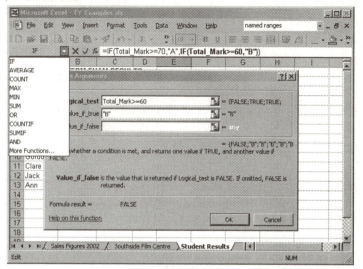

• AutoFill the functions down the column.

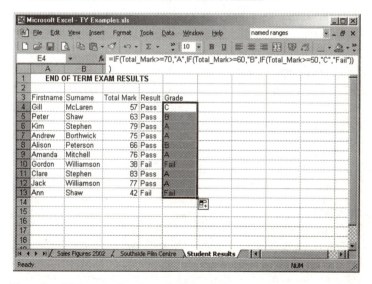

You should get A, B, C and Fail grades as appropriate. If the function does not work as expected, delete it and try again.

In this next example, the IF function is used to work out the amount of discount a customer will get on an order.

- If the order is £1000 or over, 10% will be deducted.
- If the order is between £750 and £999, 5% will be deducted.
- If the order is less than £750, no discount is given.

Enter the basic worksheet as it is displayed here. The empty columns will be completed using functions and formulas.

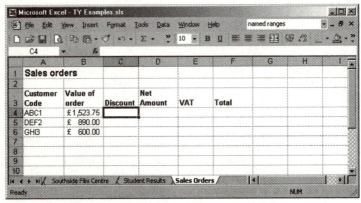

Named ranges have been created for the columns, using the Name Box.

- The Value of order column has been called *VOO*.
- The Discount column has been called *Discount*.
- The Net Amount column has been called *Net_Amount*.
- The VAT column has been called *VAT*.

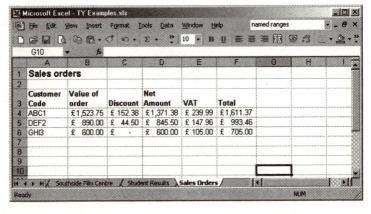

These names have been used in the functions and formulas. The formulas and functions required are displayed below.

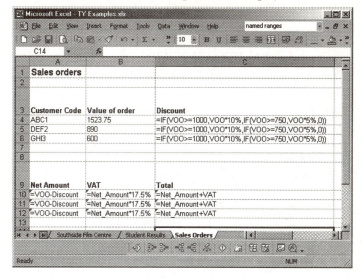

AND

The AND function returns a TRUE result if all conditions in the function are met, and a FALSE result if all conditions are not met.

For example, you may manufacture and sell traditional children's wooden toys. Your most popular items are a painted toy box, a rocking horse and building blocks. You want to keep a record of the items that customers buy from you.

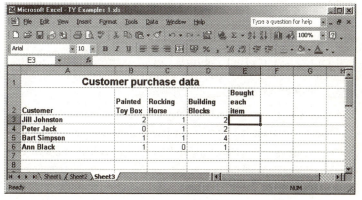

You could enter the data into a spreadsheet and use **AND** to return a TRUE value if a customer buys >0 of each item, and FALSE if they don't.

In this example, in E3, you would:

1 Click the **Insert Function** button
2 Select AND from the function list (in the **Logical** category)
3 In the **Logical1** field, insert B3>0
4 In the **Logical2** field, insert C3>0
5 In the **Logical3** field, insert D3>0
6 Click **OK**

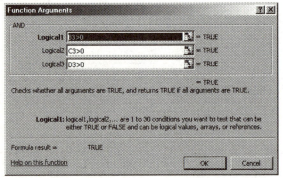

When you copy (AutoFill) the function down the column, you will get a TRUE message where ALL the conditions are met and a FALSE message where they are not.

OR

The OR function will return a TRUE value if *any* condition in the function is met, and FALSE if none are met.

You could add another column to the example used in above to identify customers who have bought more than 2 of any item that we sell.

1 Click the **Insert Function** button
2 Select OR from the function list (in the **Logical** category)
3 In the **Logical1** field, insert B3>2 to check if the value in B3 is greater than 2
4 In the **Logical2** field, insert C3>2

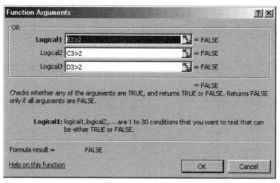

5 In the **Logical3** field, insert D3>2
6 Click **OK**

When you copy the function down the column, you will get a TRUE message where *any* condition is met and a FALSE message where none are.

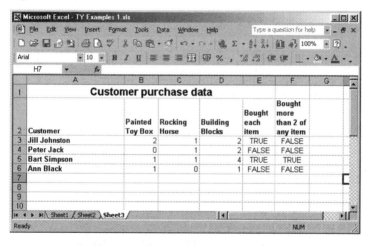

You can combine IFs and ANDs and ORs in a variety of ways.

You could use a combination of IF and AND to identify those customers who had bought at least 1 of each item, and display a message saying that they qualify for a free Teddy Bear, or perform a calculation to give a 5% discount. Your **Function Arguments** would look something like the next screenshot – with the AND function *nested* within an IF.

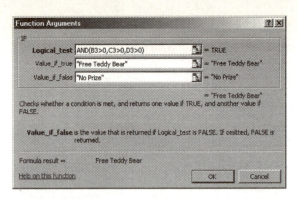

6.2 Statistical and Math functions

COUNTIF AND SUMIF

COUNTIF looks at a list of values and calculates how many of them satisfy specified criteria. It can be used when you're checking for **one** criterion. The syntax is =COUNTIF(Range,Criteria)

1 Click the **Insert Function** button
2 Select **COUNTIF** from the list of functions

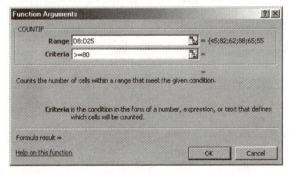

3 Enter the range of cells that you want to be counted in the **Range** field
4 Specify the criteria that must be met for an entry to be counted in the **Criteria** field
5 Click **OK**

The function could be used to count the number of students that obtained specific results in their exams.

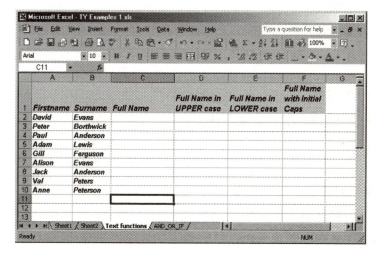

The SUMIF function works in a similar way to the COUNTIF, but adds the values together if the condition is met.

6.3 Text functions

There are a number of Text functions that you may find useful from time to time. They are very easy to use. You could type up a list of names and experiment using the functions discussed.

CONCATENATE

Use the CONCATENATE function to display the full name in column C.

1 Click the **Insert Function** button
2 Select the **CONCATENATE** function

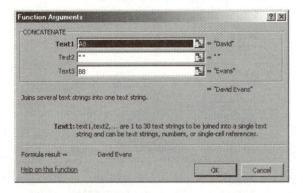

3 Enter the cell address that contains the first piece of text required in **Text1**
4 Put a space – this could be any keyboard entry – in **Text2** (inside quotation marks). If you don't put in a space, the words will run together.
5 Enter the cell address that contains the next piece of text required in **Text3**
6 Continue until all text strings have been entered – you can have up to 30 text strings
7 Click **OK**

UPPER

UPPER is a case change function. You can use it to change all the letters in a text entry to upper case.

You could use the UPPER function to display the full name in upper case in Column D.

1 Click the **Insert Function** button
2 Select the **UPPER** function

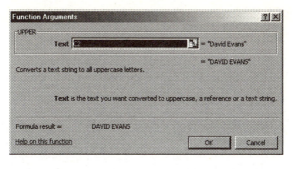

3 Enter the cell address that contains the text you want to convert e.g. **C2**

4 Click **OK**

LOWER

LOWER is a case change function. You can use it to change all the letters in a text entry to lower case.

You could use the LOWER function to display the full name in lower case in Column E.

1 Click the **Insert Function** button
2 Select the **LOWER** function

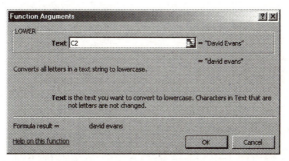

3 Enter the cell address that contains the text you want to convert e.g. C2

4 Click **OK**

PROPER

PROPER converts a text entry to initial capitals. You could use it to display the name with initial capitals in Column F.

1 Click the **Insert Function** button
2 Select the **PROPER** function

3 Enter the cell address that contains the text you want to convert e.g. C2
4 Click **OK**

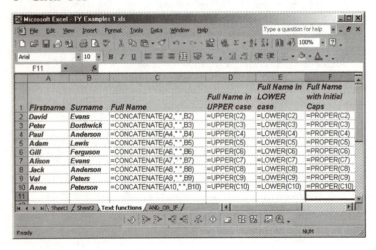

6.4 Date functions

Date functions allow you to insert the current date and/or time into a cell on your worksheet (or into calculations), and display the date and/or time in a variety of ways.

TODAY()

The TODAY() function enters the date from your computer clock into your worksheet. It's such a regularly used function that most people enter it directly through the keyboard.

To insert the current day:

1. Select a cell in your worksheet
2. Type in =**TODAY()** – you *must* type in the = and the () to get the function to work
3. Press [**Enter**]

NOW()

The NOW() function enters the date and time from your computer clock. Again, it is usually typed in through the keyboard.

To insert the current day:

1. Select a cell in your worksheet
2. Type in =**NOW()** – you *must* type in the = and the ()
3. Press [**Enter**]
- If the date and/or time are not correct when you use these functions you will need to reset the clock on your computer.

The values in the cells with the TODAY() or NOW() functions in them are *volatile*. They will be updated automatically each day as the date and time changes.

DAY, MONTH and YEAR

The **DAY**, **MONTH** and **YEAR** functions can be used to display just the section of the date required. You can use the function to return the portion required from a date entered into a cell in your worksheet, or you can nest the TODAY or NOW function within it.

To return part of a date already in a cell:

1. Select the cell that you want the DAY, MONTH or YEAR displayed in
2. Click the **Insert Function** button
3. Choose DAY, MONTH or YEAR from the function list

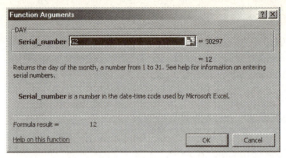

4 Enter the cell address in the **Serial_Number** field
5 Click **OK**

To enter part of the date from the TODAY() or NOW() function:

1 Select the cell that you want the DAY, MONTH or YEAR in
2 Click the **Insert Function** button
3 Choose DAY, MONTH or YEAR from the function list
4 Type TODAY() or NOW() in the **Serial_Number** field
5 Click **OK**

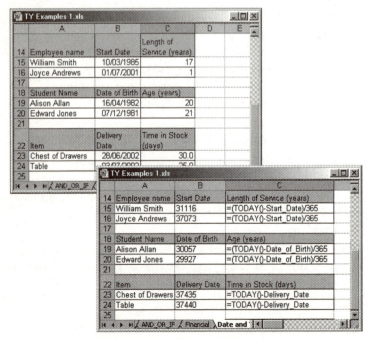

The TODAY() and NOW() functions are useful when calculating things like age, length of service, or the length of time an item has been in stock.

6.5 Financial functions

Out of the many financial functions in Excel, those dealing with loans and investments are perhaps the ones that are most useful to us all, at a personal if not professional level. Three deal with the repayment of loans (which we all have to handle at some time!), and two are useful when working with savings and investments. The arguments used in these functions are:

pv	the present (original) value of the loan
pmt	the repayment per period
rate	the interest rate per period
nper	the total number of payments

The three functions that can be used with loans are:

=PMT (**rate, nper, pv**)
calculates the payment each period if the **pv**, **rate** and **nper** are known

=RATE (**nper, pmt, pv**)
calculates the interest rate provided the **pmt**, **nper** and **pv** are known

=PV (**rate, nper, pmt**)
calculates the loan value provided **rate**, **pmt** and **nper** are known

Functions that are useful when dealing with investments are:

=FV (**rate, nper, pmt**)
calculates the final value of saving an amount (**pmt**) for a specific time (**nper**) at a given interest **rate**

=NPV (**rate, value1, value2...**)
calculates the net present value of an investment using a comparison discount rate (**rate**) and a series of future income payments from the investment (positive values) and payments to the investment (negative payments). You can have up to 29 value arguments.

Have a look at (and experiment with) these examples of how these functions can be used. You'll find other examples (and more information on these functions) in the Help system.

=PMT(rate, nper, pv)

You have decided to extend your house. Your architect estimates that it will cost £20,000. Your bank is prepared to give you a loan for this, at 10% interest per year, over 10 years. What is the monthly repayment on this loan?

You are working out a repayment, so you would use the =PMT function. The arguments would be:

=PMT(10%/12, 10*12, 20000)

10%/12 is the monthly interest repayment

10*12 is the number of repayments you will make

20000 is the amount you will borrow

Your monthly repayments would be £264.30.

=Rate (nper, pmt, pv)

What is the interest rate of a 4-year loan for £10,000 with a monthly payment (at the end of the month) of £390?

=RATE (4*12,-390, 10000)

4*12 is the number of repayments

-390 is the amount that you repay each month

10000 is the amount of the loan

The interest rate is 3%.

=PV (rate, nper, pmt)

You need to borrow some money to buy a car. You have worked out your finances, and have calculated that the most you can afford to pay back each month is £250. Your bank is willing to offer you a loan, over 4 years, at 5% interest. How much can you afford to borrow?

=PV(5%/12,4*12,-250)

5%/12 is the interest rate per month

4*12 is the number of payments over the 4 years

-250 is the amount that you pay each month

The amount you can afford to borrow is £10,855.74

=FV (rate, nper, pmt)

You inherit £10,000 that is deposited in a savings account that pays 7% annual interest. If you deposit a further £1,000 at the end of each subsequent year, what will the savings account be worth in 10 years time?

=FV(7%,10,-1000,-10000)

7% is the interest paid each year

10 is the number of payments

-1000 is the amount that you pay each year

-10000 is the initial amount deposited when you opened the account (the pv)

Your savings account will be worth £33,487.96

=NPV (rate, value1, value2...)

You have just received a windfall payment of £20,000. You have decided to invest the money into a venture which will pay you an annual income of £7,200, £8,400 and £10,400 in the next three years. The current rate of interest is 7.5%. What is the NPV of your investment.

=NPV(7.5%,-20000,7200,8400,10400)

7.5% is the interest rate

-20000 is the initial payment (negative value as you paid it in)

7200, 8400, 10400 are the amounts that you receive in the next three years (positive values as it is money you receive)

The NPV of your investment would be £2,174.94

6.6 Lookup functions

You can locate values in a table array using the HLOOKUP (horizontal) or VLOOKUP (vertical) functions. Use HLOOKUP when your comparison values are located in a row across the top of a table of data, and you want to look along a row to that column.

The format of the function is:

=HOOKUP(Lookup value, table array, row number)

You can identify the column using cell addresses or column labels.

Use VLOOKUP when your comparison values are located in a

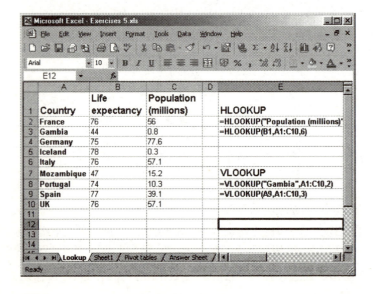

column to the left of the data you want to find, and you want to look down a column until the data is located.

=VLOOKUP(Lookup value, table array, column number)

You can identify the row using cell addresses or row labels.

6.7 Data tables

A data table is a range of values that can be substituted into a formula.

There are two types of data tables – one-variable (where one value in the formula is substituted) and two-variable (where two values in the formula are substituted).

One-variable data table

In a one-variable data table, the values can be listed down a column or across a row.

In this example, we have a distance of 4000 miles to travel, and want to work out how long it will take. We can use a one-variable data table to show us how long it will take to travel the distance. The time taken depends on the speed at which we travel (the variable). The basic formula to calculate the time it takes will be Distance/Speed.

1 Enter the distance that you need to travel in a cell
2 Enter the variable data (the speeds that you could average each hour) either across one row or down one column

	A	B	C	D	E
1	Column-Orientated Data Table				
2	Distance	4000	miles	Speed (input cell)	40
3	Speed (input values)/miles per hour	Hours taken			
4		100			
5	40	100			
6	50	80			
7	60	67			
8	70	57			

Column-orientated table:

1 Type the formula that refers to the input cell in the row above the first value and one cell to the right of the column of values. Type any additional formulas to the right of the first formula.

2 Select the range of cells that contain the formulas *and* values that you want to substitute
3 On the **Data** menu, click **Table**
4 Type the cell reference for the input cell in the **Column input cell** box

	A	B	C	D	E
1	Column-Orientated Data				
2	Distance	4000	miles	Speed (input	40
3	Speed (input values)/miles per hour	Hours taken			
4		=B2/E2			
5	40	=TABLE(,E2)			
6	50	=TABLE(,E2)			
7	60	=TABLE(,E2)			
8	70	=TABLE(,E2)			

Row-oriented table:

1 Type the formula in the column to the left of the first value and one cell below the row of values. Type any additional formulas below the first formula.
2 Select the range of cells that contain the formulas and values you want to substitute
3 On the **Data** menu, click **Table**
4 Type the cell reference for the input cell in the **Row input cell** box

Two-variable data table

A two-variable input table is very similar, but with a row and a column input value.

You could create a two-variable input table to calculate the 'times tables' from 1 to 12.

1 Enter the formula that refers to the two input cells in a cell on the worksheet (in B4 in this example)
2 Enter one list of input values in the same column, below the formula

	A	B	C	D	E	F	G	H	I	J	K	L	M	N
1		Table	1											
2		Number	1											
3								Table						
4			1	2	3	4	5	6	7	8	9	10	11	12
5		1	1	2	3	4	5	6	7	8	9	10	11	12
6		2	2	4	6	8	10	12	14	16	18	20	22	24
7		3	3	6	9	12	15	18	21	24	27	30	33	36
8		4	4	8	12	16	20	24	28	32	36	40	44	48
9	N	5	5	10	15	20	25	30	35	40	45	50	55	60
10	u	6	6	12	18	24	30	36	42	48	54	60	66	72
11	m	7	7	14	21	28	35	42	49	56	63	70	77	84
12	b	8	8	16	24	32	40	48	56	64	72	80	88	96
13	e	9	9	18	27	36	45	54	63	72	81	90	99	108
14	r	10	10	20	30	40	50	60	70	80	90	100	110	120
15		11	11	22	33	44	55	66	77	88	99	110	121	132
16		12	12	24	36	48	60	72	84	96	108	120	132	144

3 Enter the second list of input values in the same row, to the right of the formula
4 Select the range of cells that contains the formula and both the row and column of values (B4:N16)
5 Open the **Data** menu, and choose **Table**
6 In the **Row input cell** box, enter the reference to the input cell for the input values in the row
7 In the **Column input cell** box, enter the reference to the input cell for the input values in the column
8 Click **OK**

	B	C	D	E	F
1	Table	1			
2	Number	1			
3					
4	=C1*C2	1	2	3	4
5	1	=TABLE(C1,C2)	=TABLE(C1,C2)	=TABLE(C1,C2)	=TABLE(C1,C2)
6	2	=TABLE(C1,C2)	=TABLE(C1,C2)	=TABLE(C1,C2)	=TABLE(C1,C2)
7	3	=TABLE(C1,C2)	=TABLE(C1,C2)	=TABLE(C1,C2)	=TABLE(C1,C2)
8	4	=TABLE(C1,C2)	=TABLE(C1,C2)	=TABLE(C1,C2)	=TABLE(C1,C2)
9	5	=TABLE(C1,C2)	=TABLE(C1,C2)	=TABLE(C1,C2)	=TABLE(C1,C2)
10	6	=TABLE(C1,C2)	=TABLE(C1,C2)	=TABLE(C1,C2)	=TABLE(C1,C2)
11	7	=TABLE(C1,C2)	=TABLE(C1,C2)	=TABLE(C1,C2)	=TABLE(C1,C2)
12	8	=TABLE(C1,C2)	=TABLE(C1,C2)	=TABLE(C1,C2)	=TABLE(C1,C2)
13	9	=TABLE(C1,C2)	=TABLE(C1,C2)	=TABLE(C1,C2)	=TABLE(C1,C2)
14	10	=TABLE(C1,C2)	=TABLE(C1,C2)	=TABLE(C1,C2)	=TABLE(C1,C2)
15	11	=TABLE(C1,C2)	=TABLE(C1,C2)	=TABLE(C1,C2)	=TABLE(C1,C2)
16	12	=TABLE(C1,C2)	=TABLE(C1,C2)	=TABLE(C1,C2)	=TABLE(C1,C2)

♦ Go to one-variable and two-variable data tables in Help for more information.

6.8 Scenarios

A scenario is a named set of values that can be applied to a set of selected cells in your workbook. They are used when you want to set up a model where you can quickly substitute the various inputs so that you can compare the solutions. They are useful in 'What If' situations, where you can set up several named inputs and apply them to you worksheet to help identify best and worst cases.

Let's say you wanted to perform some calculations to work out the monthly repayments that you would have to make on a loan. You are considering three options.

	Amount of loan	Interest rate	Payback period
Option 1	£20,000	7%	5 years
Option 2	£25,000	7%	8 years
Option 3	£30,000	10%	12 years

You could set up each option as a scenario.

1 Set up your worksheet to show the Option 1 payments and input the formula required

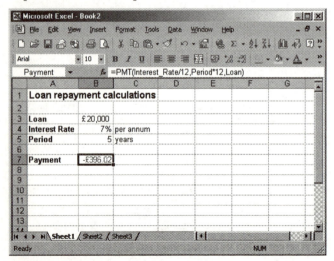

2 Open the **Tools** menu
3 Select **Scenarios...**

4 At the **Scenario Manager** dialog box click **Add...**
5 Give the scenario a name, e.g. Option 1
6 Specify the cells that will change when you show the various scenarios, e.g. B3:B5 and click **OK**
7 Type the values in for Option 1 and click **Add**

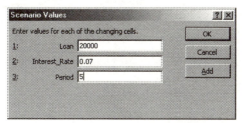

8 Repeat steps 5-7 for Option 2 and 3
9 Click **OK**

The scenarios will be listed in the Scenario Manager dialog box. If a scenario is wrong or no longer required, you can edit or delete it from this dialog box.

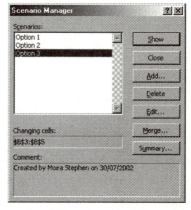

To see the repayment options, select an option and click **Show** – the values on your worksheet will be substituted by those in the scenario.

When you show each scenario in turn, you can see the outcome of applying that scenario only. If you wish to see the outcomes of all the scenarios at once (which makes it easier to compare them) you must create a scenario summary.

To create a scenario summary:

1 Display the **Scenario Manager** dialog box
2 Click **Summary...**
3 Choose **Scenario summary** as the report type and edit the **Result cells** field if necessary

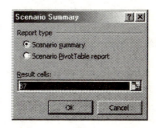

4 Click **OK**

A new worksheet will be created showing the summary report.

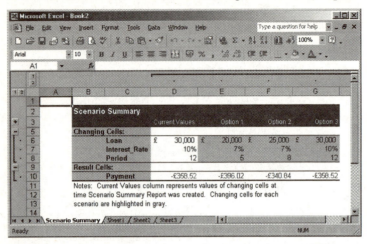

6.9 PivotTable

There may be times when you want to create a report that summarizes the data held in a worksheet. You might want to perform some calculations on the summarized data, or filter it to display specific data from the list. PivotTables can be used in this situation. They are interactive tables that allow you to summarize large amounts of data.

A PivotTable consists of four areas – page, column, row and data.

The page, column and row areas show the data that you have added to the PivotTable – they act as labels for the data that you are summarizing. They are also used to filter the data that you add.

The data area is where the summary result calculations are performed and displayed. Each item in the data area must have a function associated with it – sum, average, count etc.

PAGE	COLUMN	
	ROW	DATA

You don't *have* to have an item in the page, column or row area, but you *must* have something in the data area (you have to be summarizing something!).

In this example we've used Excel to record details of customer orders. We then go on to summarize this data using a PivotTable. We want to be able to:

- Display the order data by town
- Filter the data to show the order data from each customer
- Calculate totals for the number of each item purchased

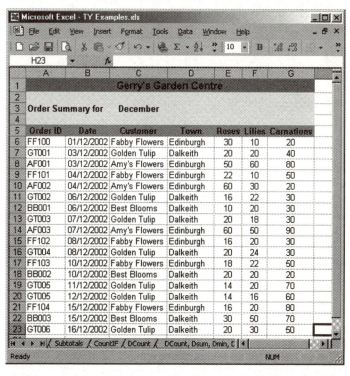

To create a PivotTable to do this:

1 Click anywhere inside the list of data for which you want to create a PivotTable
2 Open the **Data** menu and choose **PivotTable and Pivot Chart Report...**

3 Select *Microsoft Excel List or database* and *PivotTable* at step 1 of the wizard and click **Next**
4 Check the range (and edit if necessary) at step 2 of the wizard, then click **Next**
5 At step 3, choose the location for the PivotTable – if you want it in the existing worksheet, enter the cell address for the top left corner of the PivotTable

6 Click **Finish**

An empty PivotTable will be displayed, with the Field list and PivotTable toolbar displayed. You can now lay out your PivotTable onscreen.

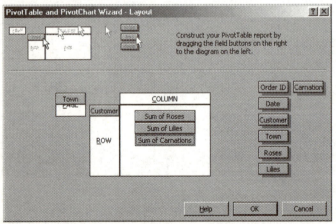

Drag the items from the field list and drop them in the area that you want them to be in on the PivotTable. Any fields that you want to be able to filter your data by should be in the Page, Column or Row fields. Date that will be summarized goes in the Data area.

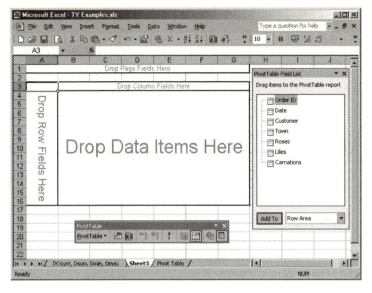

Drag the

- Town field to the Page area
- Customer to the Column area
- Roses, Lilies and Carnations to the Data area
- Close the field list

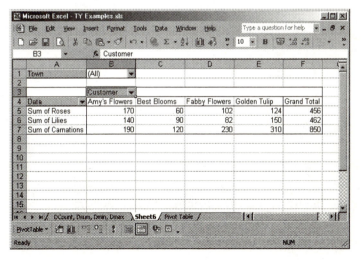

- You can *pivot* the data in your PivotTable by dragging the fields from one area to another – watch the mouse pointer as you do this – it gives you a clue as to what area you are over!
- *Filter* your data using the drop-down arrows at the Page, Row and Column area.

This section has given you an introduction to PivotTables – experiment with them and visit the Help system for more information.

Summary

In this chapter we have discussed some of the many functions available in Excel. We have introduced:

- Logical functions – IF, AND, OR.
- Statistical and math functions – COUNTIF and SUMIF.
- Text functions – concatenate, upper, lower, proper.
- Date functions – today, now, day, month, and year.
- Financial functions that are used when dealing with loans and investments.
- Lookup functions.
- Data Tables.
- Scenarios.
- PivotTables.

07 charting and drawing

In this unit you will learn

- how to produce charts from your data
- about printing charts
- how to add special effects to your charts
- about the Drawing tools

Aims of this chapter

Pictures often speak louder than words (and numbers). This chapter discusses Excel's excellent charting capabilities – they're easy to use and look great. We'll also take a look at the drawing toolbar, and see how it can be used to enhance your charts (and data). Have fun!

7.1 Preparing your data

Excel can create charts – bar graphs, line graphs, pie charts, scatter diagrams, etc. – from the data in your worksheet.

You can create your chart on the same worksheet as the data on which the chart is built (an embedded chart), or on a separate chart sheet.

- *Ideally* the data should be in adjacent cells.
- If there are blank rows or columns within the data to be charted, remove these before you try to chart it.

To chart data that is not in adjacent cells:

1 Select the first group of cells you want to chart

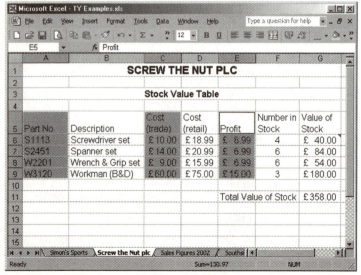

2 Hold the [Ctrl] key down while you click and drag over the other groups you want to include in your chart

* When the non-adjacent cells are selected, the areas *must* be able to combine to form a rectangle.

7.2 Chart Wizard

The Chart Wizard is used to step you through the process of setting up your chart.

To chart the data in your worksheet:

1 Select the data you want to chart – including the column headings and row labels

2 Click the **Chart Wizard** tool on the Standard toolbar

3 At Step 1 of the Chart Wizard, select the **Chart type**

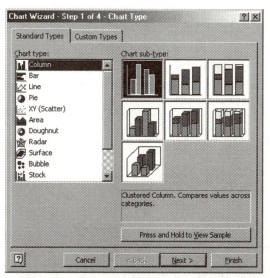

There are over a dozen basic chart types and unlimited variations

4 Click the **Press and Hold to View Sample** button to see what your data would look like in your chosen chart type

5 Once you've decided on a type, click **Next**

6 At Step 2, on the **Data Range** tab, check the data range selected, decide whether you want to display the data series

in rows or columns (try both and decide which you prefer). Click **Next**.

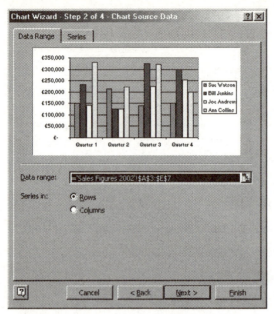

- Once a chart has been created, changes made to the data on which the chart is based, will automatically be reflected in the chart. This happens regardless of whether the chart is an object in your worksheet, or on a separate chart sheet.

7 At Step 3, explore the various tabs in the **Chart Options** dialog box and select the options you require. Click **Next**.

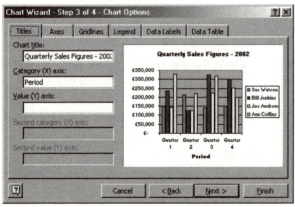

8 Decide where the chart should be located – in your worksheet, or on a separate chart sheet. Click **Finish**.

Using Wizards

Click `Next >` to move to the next step, `< Back` to return to the previous, `Cancel` if you change your mind and want to abandon the Wizard, and `Finish` when you're done.

7.3 A chart in your worksheet

Once you've created a chart, the Chart toolbar will be displayed.

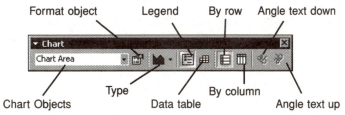

The chart will be selected – indicated by handles in each corner and along each side.

If you click on the worksheet area, the chart becomes deselected, and the Chart toolbar disappears.

To select the chart again, click on it once. The **Chart** menu appears in the menu bar when the chart is selected.

Chart objects

Each area of a chart is an object – you have a chart area object, plot area object, category axis object, legend object, etc.

To select a chart object:

- Choose the object from the **Chart Objects** list [Legend].

Or

- Click on the object you want to select.

Move, resize and delete charts

If you want to move, resize or delete a chart that is an object on a worksheet, you must first select the Chart Area – either point to the chart area within the chart and click (a prompt will tell you what the mouse is pointing at) or choose Chart Area from the Chart Objects list on the Chart toolbar.

To move the chart:

1. Select the chart
2. Point to the chart area using the mouse – a prompt will appear to tell you what area you are pointing at
3. Drag the chart to its new position

To resize the chart:

1. Select the chart
2. Point to one of the handles along the edge of the chart area
3. Drag the handle to increase or decrease the size of the object

To delete the chart:

1. Select the chart
2. Press the [**Delete**] key on your keyboard

Formatting chart objects

You can change the formatting of each object in your chart to get the effect you want.

To format an object in your chart:

1. Choose the object required from the **Chart Objects** list
2. Click the **Format** tool on the Chart toolbar

Or

- Double-click the chart object you want to format.

When the **Format** dialog box appears, explore it to see the formatting options you have. Experiment with the options until you find the right formatting for your chart. For example:

- To change the position of the legend, double-click on it, then use the **Placement** tab in the **Format** dialog box.
- To change the colour of the plot area, double-click on it, then select the colour required from the dialog box.
- To remove or edit the gridlines, double-click on them, then use the **Patterns** or **Scale** tabs to specify your requirements.
- If you want to format the font of an object, use the tools on the Formatting toolbar – font, size, bold, italic, etc.

To change the chart type

If your chart doesn't look the way you expected, and you think a different chart type would be better, you can change the type at any time.

To change the chart type:

1 Click the drop-down arrow to the right of the **Chart Type** tool on the Chart toolbar
2 Select the type of chart required

Other options

If you explore the menus when your chart is selected, you will find that some of the worksheet menu options have disappeared, and options specific to charting have appeared. The **Format** and **Chart** menus contain most of the charting options.

In the Chart menu choose:

- **Chart Type...** to return to the dialog box displayed at Step 1 of the Wizard. This gives you access to all the chart types and sub-types.
- **Source Data...** to return to Step 2 of the Wizard. If you need to edit the data range, this is the best place to do it.
- **Chart Options...** to return to the options at Step 3. You can add titles, change the position of the legend, edit the gridlines, etc. through this dialog box.
- **Location...** to return to the dialog box displayed at Step 4 of the Wizard. You can change the location of the selected chart from here – useful if you want to move it to another sheet, or decide to put it on a separate chart sheet.

7.4 A chart on a separate sheet

If you opt to locate your chart in a new sheet, your chart will be displayed on a sheet called *Chart1* (unless you've already got a Chart1 sheet, in which case it will be in the Chart2 sheet or Chart3 sheet). The chart sheet is inserted to the left of the worksheet from which it gets its data.

The Chart toolbar is displayed when the chart sheet is selected. You can use the Chart toolbar, or the **Format** or **Chart** menu to modify the chart as required.

You can rename the sheet, move it to another location in your workbook, or delete it if you decide you don't need it any more (see Chapter 4 for renaming, moving and deleting sheets).

7.5 Charts without the Wizard

Charts can be created very quickly, missing out the steps you work through with the Chart Wizard. The charts created use the default chart layout – this is a column chart (unless it has been changed on your machine – see section 7.7).

To create an embedded chart:

1 Select the cells you want to chart
2 Click the **Default Chart** tool – if the tool it not displayed, you can add it to a toolbar (see Chapter 11).
3 Drag the chart into position on the sheet

To create a chart on a separate chart sheet:

1 Select the cells you want to chart
2 Press [**F11**]

The charts you create can be formatted and printed in the same way as those created using the Chart Wizard.

7.6 Printing your chart

You can print your chart with or without the data on which it is based. To print a chart that is an object within a worksheet you have several options. I suggest you check it through Print Preview before you print.

To print out all of the data on the worksheet and the chart:

- Print the worksheet as normal (with the chart deselected).

To get a printout of the chart only:

- Select the chart on the worksheet, then print.

To get the chart, plus its data, but no other data from the worksheet:

- Select the chart and click the **Data Table** tool on the Chart toolbar to display the data table for the chart. Print out with the chart selected.

To print a chart that is on a separate chart sheet:

1. Select the chart sheet
2. Print as usual

- If you also want to print out the data on which the chart is based, display the data table before you print.

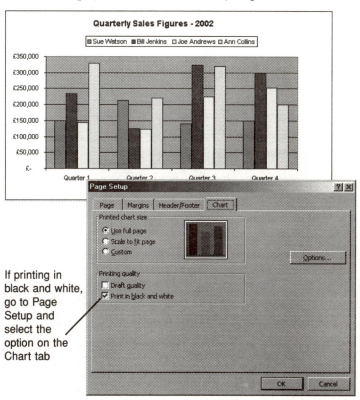

If printing in black and white, go to Page Setup and select the option on the Chart tab

7.7 Default chart

The default chart in Excel is a column chart. If you don't use column charts very often, you can change the default chart type.

To change the default chart type:

1 Open the **Chart** menu and choose **Chart Type...**
2 Select the chart type and subtype you want as your default
3 Click the **Set as default chart** button

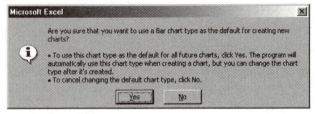

4 Click **Yes** to change the default type, **No** to cancel the change.

7.8 Special effects

One of the best ways to find out about the charting capabilities is to experiment. However, here are some tips and pointers if you want to get that little bit more from your charts!

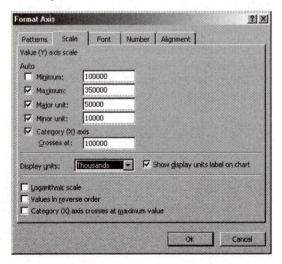

Value (Y-axis) scale

By default, the value axis starts at 0. If you don't have any small values to plot e.g. if all your values are 100,000 and over, this results in a large 'dead' area at the bottom of your chart. You can get rid of this area if you set an appropriate minimum value for the axis.

1 Double-click the value axis
2 Amend the values on the **Scale** tab as required
3 Click **OK**

• You can also amend the Display units setting from this tab.

Overlaps and Gap Widths

The spacing between each bar or column on a chart is called the 'overlap'. The space between each group of bars or columns is the 'gap width'. You can adjust this setting from the **Format Data Series** dialog box.

1 Double-click any data series to open the **Format Data Series** dialog box
2 Select the **Options** tab
3 Set the **Overlap** and/or **Gap** settings as required
4 Click **OK**

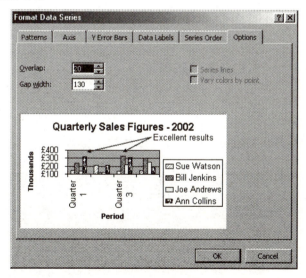

Picture series

If you explore the **Patterns** tab in the **Format Data Series** dialog box you will find lots of colours and effects that you can use for each data series if you wish.

If you want a very special effect however, you could consider putting a *picture* into a data series – perhaps a £ or € symbol, or a pile of currency!

To display a picture in the data series:

1 Insert a picture from ClipArt or Microsoft Gallery into your worksheet (check out the on-line Help if necessary)
2 Copy the picture (select it and click the **Copy** tool)
3 Select the series that you want the picture displayed in
4 Click **Paste**

Combined charts

You can customize your charts further by combining some chart types (you can't combine all types – experiment with them).

To combine a column chart with a line chart:

1 Display a column chart in 2-D (**Chart Type** tool)
2 Select the series that you wish to display as a line
3 Choose **Line Chart** from the **Chart Type** list

7.9 Drawing tools

You can use the Drawing toolbar to add different effects to your charts (and data). If you want to draw an arrow pointing to an object within your chart, and attach a message to the arrow, you must use the drawing tools.

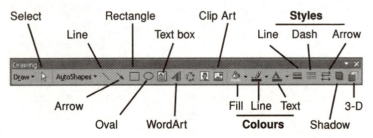

To display the Drawing toolbar:

- Click the Drawing tool on the Standard toolbar.

Line, Arrow, Rectangle and Oval

The basic tools are the Line, Arrow, Rectangle and Oval. You can use these tools to draw basic lines and shapes.

To use these tools:

1 Click the tool
2 Click and drag to draw the shape

For a perfect square or circle, select the Rectangle or Oval tool, and hold down [**Shift**] as you click and drag.

To do any work on an object, you must select it first, then deselect when you have done.

To resize or move your drawing objects:

1 Click and drag a 'handle' to resize the object
2 Click and drag within the object to move it

To add a shadow or 3-D effect to your object:

1 Click the **Shadow** tool ▣ or **3-D** tool ▣
2 Choose the effect you want

To change a line or arrow style of an object:

1 Click the **Line** ▣, **Dash** ▣ or **Arrow Style** tool ▣
2 Choose the effect you want from the drop-down list

To change the fill colour, line colour or font colour of an object:

1 Click the drop-down arrow to the right of the **Fill** ▣ or **Line Color** tool ▣ or the **Font Color** tool ▣.
2 Choose a colour

To delete a drawing object:

- Press [**Delete**] on your keyboard.

Text boxes

You can add text anywhere if it is contained within a Text box.

To insert a Text box:

1 Click the **Text box** tool
2 Click and drag within the document to create the Text box
3 Type in the text and format it if required
4 Click outside the Text box to end

AutoShapes

If you want to draw stars, banners, block arrows, flow chart symbols, etc. you may find the shape you need in the AutoShapes. These are just as easy to use as the basic shapes above.

1 Click the **AutoShapes** tool
2 Choose a category
3 Select a shape
4 Click and drag to draw your shape

♦ **Callouts** are a variation on Text Boxes and work in the same way – see above.

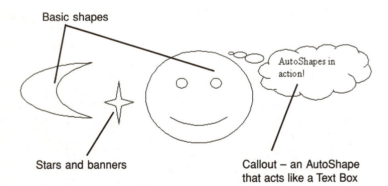

7.10 Some more options

Draw on the Drawing toolbar gives access to more options.

Grouping

If you are drawing a picture using different drawing objects, you will find that your final picture is easier to resize and move if you *Group* the objects together.

Before you can group several objects, you must select them.

To select more than one object at a time:

1 Select the first object required – click on it
2 Hold the [**Shift**] key down while you click on each of the other objects

Or

1 Click the **Select Objects** tool on the Drawing toolbar
2 Click and drag over the objects you want to select

To group objects:

1 Select the objects you want to group
2 Click the drop-down arrow to the right of **Draw** on the Drawing toolbar
3 Choose **Group**

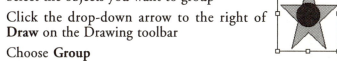

The objects are grouped together into one object and can then be resized, moved or deleted as one. If you need to work on an individual object that has been grouped, you can ungroup the object again.

To ungroup an object:

1 Select the object you want to ungroup
2 Click the drop-down arrow to the right of **Draw**
3 Choose **Ungroup**
4 Deselect the objects

To regroup objects that have been ungrouped:

1 Click the drop-down arrow to the right of **Draw**
2 Choose **Regroup**

Bring Forward, Send Backward

When you draw your objects on top of each other, the first one you draw is on the lowest layer, the second one is on a layer above the first one, the third one on the next layer and so on.

If your objects are on the wrong layer relative to each other, you can move them backwards and forwards through the layers as necessary.

To move an object from one layer to another:

1 Select the object
2 Choose **Order** from the **Draw** options
3 Move the object backwards or forwards as required

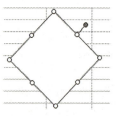

- **Bring to Front** and **Send to Back** move the object to the top or bottom layer respectively.
- **Bring Forward** and **Send Backward** move the object one layer at a time.

Rotate and Flip

Objects can be rotated left or right 90°, or freely through any angle, or flipped horizontally or vertically.

To rotate an object:

1 Select the object
2 Click and drag the rotate handle (small green circle) until the object is in the position required

To flip an object:

1 Select the object
2 Choose **Rotate or Flip** from the Draw options
3 Select a rotate or flip option

You can use the drawing tools to create different effects on your worksheet data and charts. If you create charts, try using an Arrow and a Text Box to add emphasis to it!

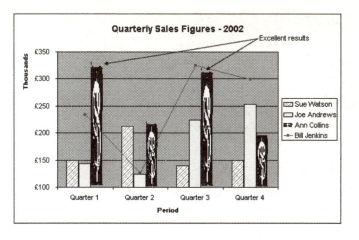

Summary

In this chapter we have discussed some of the options available when creating and editing charts in Excel. We have discussed:

- Preparing data for charting.
- The Chart Wizard.
- Charts embedded in worksheets.
- Charts on separate sheets.
- Producing charts without using the Chart Wizard.
- Printing charts.
- Changing the default chart.
- Special effects on charts.
- The Drawing toolbar.
- Manipulating drawn objects

08
autoformat, styles and templates

In this unit you will learn
- how to format your data using AutoFormat
- how to use, create and edit Styles
- about workbook and worksheet templates

Aims of this chapter

In this chapter we will discuss some of the ways you can automate the formatting and page layout of your worksheet. We considered several formatting and page layout options in Chapter 3. In this chapter we will discuss how AutoFormat, Styles and Templates can make you more efficient when formatting.

8.1 AutoFormat

Instead of formatting your worksheet manually (as discussed in Chapter 3), you could try the AutoFormats. The AutoFormats are layouts that are already set up in Excel, and they can be applied to any area of your worksheet.

If you don't select an area of your worksheet before applying an AutoFormat, Excel will apply the AutoFormat to everything surrounding the current cell, until it reaches an empty row and/or column.

If you want to apply the AutoFormat to an area that includes empty rows and/or columns, make sure you select the whole area first.

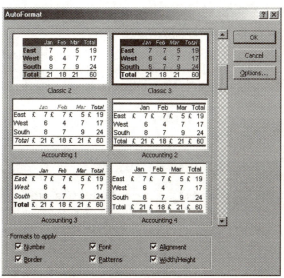

To apply an AutoFormat:

1 Select the area (if necessary)
2 Open the **Format** menu and choose **AutoFormat…**
3 Scroll through the list and choose a format
4 Click the **Options** button and deselect any options you don't want to apply
5 Click **OK**

8.2 Introducing styles

A style is a set of formatting options that you save as a group. When you want to apply the formats held in a style, you apply the style rather than each formatting option individually.

If you don't apply a style to the text or data you enter into your worksheet, it is formatted using the Normal style.

If you format your data using the Currency, Comma Style or Percent style tools on the Formatting toolbar you are applying a style that has already been set up in Excel. Other predefined styles are: Currency (0 decimal places), Comma (0 decimal places), Followed Hyperlink and Hyperlink. These styles can be located in the Style dialog box (see section 8.3) or through the Style tool which can be added to the toolbar (see Chapter 11).

Using styles has two main benefits:

- Consistency – when you apply a style, all the formatting options contained within it are applied in one go (you won't accidentally use the wrong font size or colour).
- Speed – it's usually quicker to apply a style than to apply formatting options using the Format Cells dialog box.

8.3 Working with styles

You can apply existing styles to your cells, edit existing styles, create styles of your own and delete styles you no longer use.

To apply an existing style:

1 Select the range of cells you want to format

2. Choose **Style...** from the **Format** menu
3. Select the style you want to use from the **Style name** list
4. Click **OK**

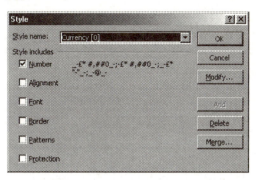

- You can click the style tools on the Formatting toolbar to apply currency 🖲 comma , and % percent styles.

To modify an existing style:

1. Choose **Style...** from the **Format** menu
2. Select the style to modify from the **Style name** list
3. Click the **Modify...** button
4. Make the changes required in the **Format Cells** dialog box
5. Click **OK** to return to the Style dialog box
6. Click **OK** to return to your worksheet

To create a new style:

1. Choose **Style...** from the **Format** menu
2. Enter a new name for the style in the **Style name** list
3. Work through steps 3–5 above to define the style
4. Click **Add** to add the style to the list *without* applying the style to the selected cell, then click **Close**

Or

5. Click **OK** to add the style to the list and apply it to the selected cell

To delete a style:

1. Choose **Style...** from the **Format** menu

2. Select the style you want to delete from the **Style name** list
3. Click the **Delete** button
4. Click **OK**

- You cannot delete the Normal style.
- If you delete the Currency, Comma or Percent style, you will not be able to use their tools on the Formatting toolbar.

If you have styles already set up in one workbook, and decide you want to use them in another workbook, you can copy the styles over.

To copy styles from one workbook to another:

1. Open the workbook that contains the styles you want to copy
2. Open the workbook that you want to copy the styles into
3. Choose **Style...** from the **Format** menu
4. Click the **Merge** button
5. Double-click the workbook that contains the styles you want to copy

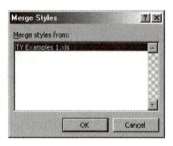

- If the destination workbook already contains styles of the same name as those being copied in, you will be asked to confirm whether or not you want the styles copied.

6. Click **OK**

- Styles can be applied and edited from the Style tool. If you intend to use styles, I suggest you add the Style tool to one of your toolbars (see section 11.4).

8.4 Workbook templates

A template is the pattern on which your workbook or worksheet is based. Up until now, your workbooks have been based on the default template. This is the one used to create a new workbook when you start Excel, or when you click the **New** tool on the Standard toolbar, or choose **Workbook** from the **General** tab in the **Templates** dialog box.

If you intend to create different workbooks that follow the same basic layout, you could create a *custom* template for them. The template would contain the standard elements of your workbooks, e.g. standard text, column and row headings, formulas, headers/footers, styles, etc.

To create a custom workbook template:

1. Create a new workbook
2. Insert or delete sheets as necessary to get the number of sheets you require in this template
3. Add any standard text, formatting, formulas, functions, headers/footers, styles, etc. to the workbook
4. If you want a preview of your workbook to be displayed in the New dialog box, choose **Properties** from the **File** menu. On the **Summary** tab in the Properties dialog box, select the **Save preview picture** checkbox and click **OK**
5. Click the **Save** tool on the Standard toolbar
6. In the **Save as type** field, choose *Template*
7. Select the *Templates* folder in the **Save in** field
8. Type in a name for the template in the **File name** field
9. Click **Save**
10. Close your template when you've finished

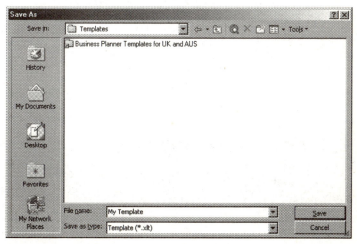

To create a new workbook using your custom template:

1. Choose **New** from the **File** menu
2. Click **General Templates** on the Task Pane
3. Select a template from the **General** tab in the **Templates** dialog box
4. Click **OK**

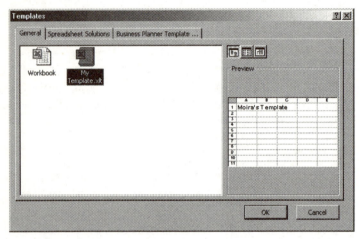

If you want to make a custom workbook template the default workbook template, you can do so.

To create the default workbook template:

1. Follow steps 1–6 on page 149
2. Select the *XLStart* folder – usually located in C:\Windows\Application Data\Microsoft\Excel\XLStart
3. In the **File name** field, type 'Book' (this is the template name Excel will look for when it starts up)
4. Click **Save**
5. Close your template when you've finished

If you decide not to use your own workbook template as the default, remove it from the *XLStart* folder. Templates are normally stored in C:\Windows\Application Data\Microsoft\Templates.

8.5 Worksheet templates

You can also create templates for the worksheets you add to your workbooks.

To create a custom worksheet template:

1. Create a new workbook consisting of *one* sheet only
2. Add any standard text, formatting, formulas, headers/footers, styles, etc. to the worksheet
3. If you want a preview of your worksheet to be displayed in the **Insert** dialog box, choose **Properties** from the **File** menu. On the **Summary** tab in the Properties dialog box, select the **Save preview picture** checkbox and click **OK**.
4. Click the **Save** tool on the Standard toolbar
5. In the **Save as type** field, choose *Template*
6. Select the *Templates* folder in the **Save in** field
7. Type in a name for the template in the **File name** field
8. Click **Save**
9. Close the worksheet template

To insert a custom worksheet template:

1. Right-click on the sheet tab and click **Insert...** from the shortcut menu
2. Select your worksheet template from the **General** tab in the **Insert** dialog box

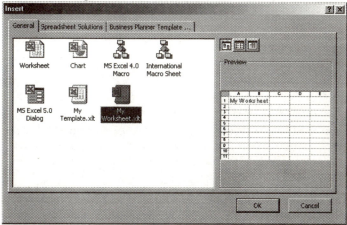

3 Click **OK**

The new sheet will be inserted to the left of the selected one.

- You can make your custom worksheet the default inserted when you insert one into a workbook. Save the worksheet as a template in the *XLStart* folder using the name '*Sheet*'.

If you later change your mind and don't want to use your own template as the default, remove it from the *XLStart* folder.

Summary

In this chapter we have discussed some of the ways you can automate the way you work in Excel. We have considered:

- Autoformat.
- Using standard Excel styles.
- Editing styles.
- Creating your own styles.
- Designing a custom workbook template.
- Creating a new workbook using your custom template.
- Changing the default workbook template.
- Creating a custom worksheet template.
- Inserting the custom worksheet template into your worksheet.

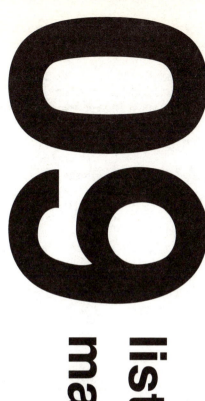

09 list management

In this unit you will learn

- how to sort data
- about filtering data
- how to validate data
- how to insert subtotals
- how to manipulate data using Database functions

Aims of this chapter

This chapter discusses how a list of data can be manipulated using basic database commands, including Sort, AutoFilter, Advanced Filter and Data validation. It then looks at subtotals and some numeric database functions.

9.1 Terminology

Lists of stock items, customer names and phone numbers, exam results, etc. can all be manipulated using the list management features in Excel. You can sort, find and filter data in lists. The functions that you can perform on a list are similar to those you would expect to carry out on a database table in Microsoft Access. Because of the similarity between list manipulation and working with database tables, database terminology is used when working with lists of data in this way.

- Each row is a **record** in your list.
- Each column is a **field**.
- The column headings are the **field names**.

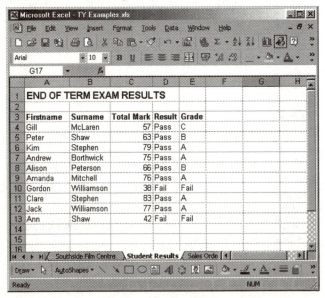

9.2 Sort

The data in your worksheet can be sorted into ascending or descending order. You can perform a simple sort, using the entries in one column only, or a more complex sort, sorting on up to three columns at a time.

When you sort your data, the block surrounding the current cell will be included in the sort – there should be no blank rows or columns inside the area you want to sort. Excel assumes that the first row of the data is a header row (with column labels) and doesn't include it in the sort.

To perform a simple sort:

1 Select any cell in the column you want to sort on

2 Click the **Sort Ascending** or **Sort Descending** tool on the Standard toolbar

Here is the student result worksheet sorted into descending order on the *Total Mark* column.

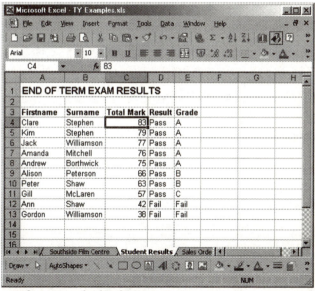

To perform a multi-level sort:

1 Select any cell within the group of cells you want sorted
2 Open the **Data** menu and choose **Sort...**

3 Select the main sort field from the **Sort by** list

4 Choose the order – **Ascending** or **Descending**

5 Select the second level sort field from the first **Then by** list, and set its sort order

6 If necessary, set the third level sort options

7 Click **OK**

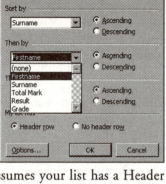

- Note that by default, Excel assumes your list has a Header row. The Header row is the row that normally contains the column labels or field names. If your list doesn't have a header row i.e. you want the first row included in the sort, select the *No header row* option.

- The list in the example below has been sorted into Surname order (ascending) then Firstname order (ascending).

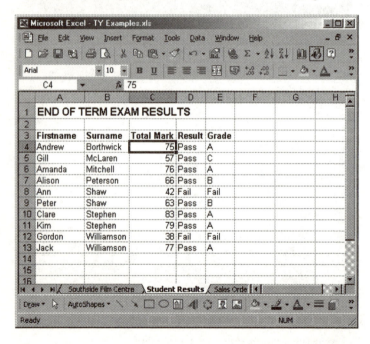

You can also use the Sort feature to rearrange the columns in your worksheet. To do this, the columns must be numbered in the order you want them to be in.

To rearrange the columns:

1 In the row immediately above (or below) your list, type in numbers to indicate the order you want the columns in
2 Select any cell in the list you want to sort
3 Open the **Data** menu and choose **Sort...**
4 Click **Options...**
5 Select **Sort left to right** in the Orientation options and click **OK**
6 In the **Sort by** field, indicate the row number that has the entries you want to sort (row 3 in this example)

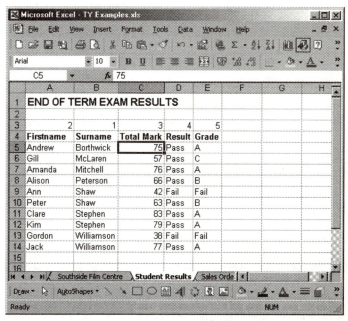

7 Click **OK**

• Once your data has been sorted, you can delete the row that contains the numbers.

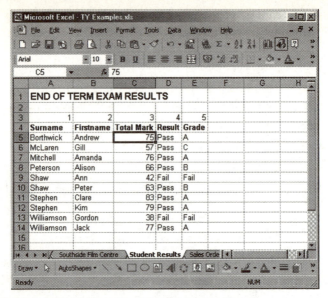

Columns rearranged in order of the numbers in Row 3

Circular references

If you try to sort columns that have formulas in them, you may run into problems with circular references where you end up with a formula in a cell that points to the cell itself. If this occurs, edit the formula to get rid of the circular reference.

If you create a circular reference, Excel will warn you and ask what you want to do about it (see section 5.6).

9.3 AutoFilter

You may want to display only the records from your list that meet specific criteria. The AutoFilter can quickly filter out the unwanted records and display only those that meet your criteria.

To switch the AutoFilter on:

1 Select a cell within the list you want to work with
2 Open the **Data** menu, choose **Filter**, then **AutoFilter**
♦ Each field name (column heading) becomes a combo box (drop-down list), with a drop-down arrow to its right.

To view records that contain a specific value:

1. Click the drop-down arrow to the right of the field name you want to select on
2. Select the value you want to view the records for
3. If you want to filter the result further, based on a value in another column, repeat steps 1 and 2 in the other column

In this example, the students who have an A in the Grade column have been selected.

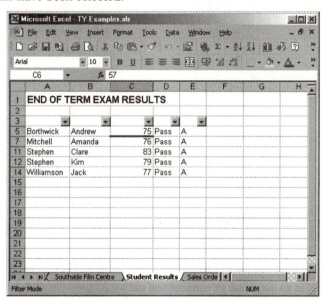

The column or columns that you have specified your criteria in have a blue arrow to the right of the field name so you can identify which columns have conditions set in them.

- By default, AutoFilter will list records that are equal to the criteria you have selected. If you want a different operator, e.g. *Does not equal*, you must use the **Custom AutoFilter** dialog box. To open the dialog box, choose **Custom...** from the drop-down list.

To display all the records again:

1. Click the drop-down arrow on the column(s) that have criteria set
2. Choose **All** from the list of options

Or

1 Open the **Data** menu and select **Filter**
2 Choose **Show All**

You can use AutoFilter to filter a list by up to two values in the same column. To do so you must set up a Custom filter.

To filter a list by two values in the same column:

1 Click the drop-down arrow to the right of the field name you want to select on
2 Select **Custom...**
3 At the **Custom AutoFilter** dialog box, set up the criteria required – in this case we are looking for students who have either a C grade or a Fail
4 Click **OK**

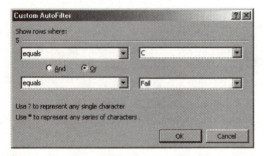

- The list of records matching your criteria will be displayed.

If you want to list all students who have more than a certain score in the *Total Mark* column, you must use the Custom AutoFilter, e.g. *Total Mark is greater than 55*. If you want all students whose surname falls within the range M–S (*Surname is greater than M*, and *Surname is less than T*), you must use the Custom AutoFilter.

To switch AutoFilter off:

1 Open the **Data** menu
2 Choose **Filter**, then **AutoFilter** to toggle the filter off

9.4 Advanced Filter

If you want to use several criteria to filter your data, or if you want to keep a set of criteria for future use, you must use the Advanced Filter. This requires you to specify the criteria you wish to apply on a separate area of the worksheet. The criteria in this range are then applied to your list of data.

Set up your criteria range first, then apply it to the list of data.

To set up the criteria range:

1 Copy the column headings or field names to a blank area in your worksheet
2 Specify the criteria required in the rows under the copied column headings

- If you enter several conditions in one row, Excel will only return a record where the first condition and the second condition and the third condition, etc. are met – in other words ALL the conditions must be met in a single record before a record is returned.

- If you enter the conditions in different rows, Excel will return a record that meets one condition or the other.

The picture below gives examples of valid criteria.

	Surname	Firstname	Total Mar	Result	Grade
		Stephen			
		Shaw			
	Surname	Firstname	Total Mar	Result	Grade
	>=M		>=70		
	Surname	Surname	Firstname	Total Mar	Result	Grade
	>=A	<=N				
	Surname	Firstname	Total Mar	Result	
	Shaw			<>Fail	

- The first one will list only those who have the surname Stephen OR Shaw.
- The second one will list all whose surname falls between M and the end of the alphabet, AND have 70 or more in the Total Mark column.
- The third one lists all whose surname starts with a letter between A and N.
- The fourth one lists all the Shaws who have not failed.

To apply the conditions set in the criteria range:

1 Select any cell in the list you want to extract records from
2 From the **Data** menu choose **Filter**, then **Advanced Filter**

3 Do you want to filter the list in place, or copy the records that match the criteria to a separate area of the worksheet – select the option required
4 Specify the range you want to extract records from (Excel should suggest the range you have selected a cell in – correct the range if necessary)
5 Indicate the cells that hold the field names and the criteria you want applied. Do not include any blank rows in the criteria area
6 If you want the result in a different location from the original list, give the cell reference of the top left corner of the area you want the result to appear in the **Copy to:** field.
7 Click **OK**

If you opted to filter the list in place, to display all the records again:

- Open the **Data** menu, choose **Filter** then select **Show All**.

9.5 Data validation

When entering data into a worksheet, you will want to try to ensure, as far as is practicable, that the data is accurate. To help achieve this, you can set up validation rules for any cell or range of cells where you want to check the validity of the data entered.

By default, each cell in your worksheet will accept any value you enter into it. However, you can limit the range of acceptable entries by setting up validation rules. Let's say, in our *Student Results* example, that we set a validation rule for the data area in the *Total Mark* column so that it would accept values between 0 and 100 only. Anything over 100, or less than 0, would not be accepted and an error message would appear.

To set a validation rule:

1 Select the cell or cells you want the rule to apply to (do not include the column heading or any other cells)
2 Open the **Data** menu and choose **Validation…**
3 On the **Settings** tab, complete the validation criteria fields

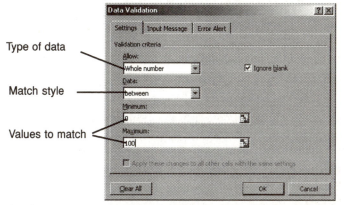

Type of data

Match style

Values to match

4 If you want a message displayed when the cell is selected, enter it on the **Input Message** tab

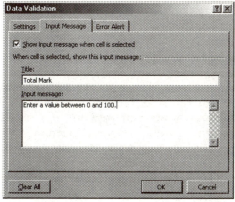

5 If you want a specific message to appear when the rule is not met, enter it on the **Error Alert** tab (a default message appears if you don't set up your own)

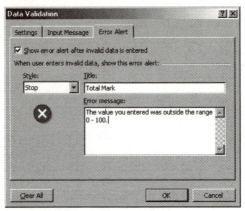

6 Click **OK** when you're finished

- When you select a cell that has the validation rule applied to it, the input message will be displayed.
- If you enter invalid data into a cell that has a validation rule applied to it, the message you set up on the **Error Alert** tab (or the default Error Alert message) will appear.

To remove a validation rule from your cells:

1 Select the cell or cells you want to remove the rule from
2 Open the **Data** menu and choose **Validation...**
3 Click the **Clear All** button
4 Click **OK**

9.6 Data form

As an alternative to displaying the data in your worksheet as a list, you may find a form easier to work with. A form displays one record, or row, from your list at a time, rather than as many records as will fit on your screen.

To display your data in a form:

1 Select any cell in the list of data you want to display in a form

2 Open the **Data** menu and choose **Form…**

The first record in the list of data will be displayed.

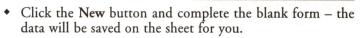

Fields that you can enter data into or edit are displayed as Text Boxes – *Firstname, Surname* and *Total Mark* in this example.

Calculated fields have their value displayed, but you cannot enter or edit the entry in them directly.

To add a new record:

- Click the **New** button and complete the blank form – the data will be saved on the sheet for you.

To delete a record:

- Display the record you want to delete and click the **Delete** button. Confirm the deletion at the prompt if you are sure that you want to go ahead and remove the record.

If you edit the contents of a field, then realize that you shouldn't have, you can restore the fields to recover the data that they contained when you accessed the record. This only works if you have *not* left the record. If you make changes, go to another record, then go back to the record you edited, you will have to manually update the fields again.

To restore a record:

- Click the **Restore** button on the form.

To move from one record to another:

- Click the **Find Prev** or **Find Next** buttons to move back and forward through the records.

To display records that meet specific criteria:

1 Click the **Criteria** button on the form
2 Complete the fields with the criteria you want to apply
3 Click the **Form** button to leave the **Criteria** dialog box
4 Use **Find Prev** or **Find Next** to move through the records that meet the criteria specified

To cancel the criteria

1 Display the **Criteria**
2 Click **Clear**
3 Click the **Form** button to leave the **Criteria** dialog box

To return to your worksheet:

♦ Click the **Close** button.

9.7 Subtotals

Lists of data can easily be summarized automatically using Subtotals. In this example, customers buy stems of flowers from a garden centre. The garden centre wants to know the total value of orders from each customer over the period. The total cost of each order has been calculated using a formula – see the Formula bar in the illustration.

To display subtotals showing the total value of the orders from each customer:

1 Sort the data into ascending order on the field that you want to create subtotals after, e.g. *Customer*

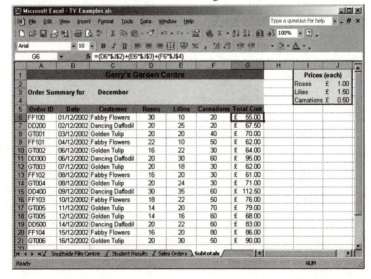

2 Select any cell within the data you wish to create subtotals for
3 Open the **Data** menu, choose **Subtotals**
4 In the **At each change in:** field, select the item you wish to subtotal on – Customer in this example

5 Select the function required from the **Use function:** list (Sum if you want subtotals)
6 In the **Add subtotal to:** list tick the box to indicate where you want the subtotal displayed
7 Select/deselect the checkboxes as required
8 Click **OK**

The result is a list showing the data grouped and subtotalled as requested.

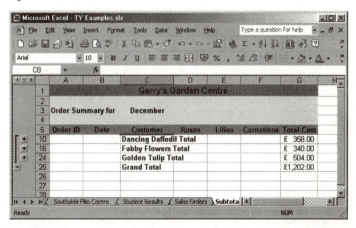

The outline pane on the left can be used to expand and collapse the level of detail required. In the example here, Level 1 = Grand Total, Level 2 = Item Subtotal, Level 3 = Detail.

You can display the amount of detail required by clicking the level numbers at the top of the pane.

- You can collapse and expand individual groups within the list by clicking the Hide ■ and Show ♦ buttons in the outline pane.
- You can show/hide the outline with the command **Data > Group and Outline > Clear Outline/Auto Outline**.

9.8 Database functions

DCOUNT

DCOUNT looks at a list of values, finds the rows that satisfy specific criteria, and counts them. It's used when you want to count the values that match >1 criteria.

Set up a criteria range – see section 9.4, Advanced Filter.

To insert the DCOUNT function:

1 Select the cell that you want the answer to appear in
2 Click the **Insert Function** button and choose **DCOUNT** from the function lists

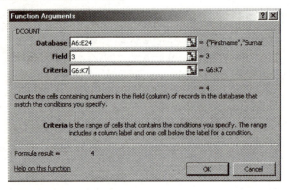

3 Enter the range of cells that your list of data fills in the **Database** field
4 For the **Field**, enter a column label or number that you want Excel to base its count on (this must be a numeric column)
5 Specify the range that the **Criteria** are in
6 Click **OK**

DSUM, DMIN, DMAX

Other functions that work along the same principle are DSUM, DMIN and DMAX.

In this example, a company takes orders for cut flowers from shops and Excel is used to keep details of the orders. Summary data could be produced using the database functions. Experiment with these (following the steps as for DCOUNT, but substituting the appropriate function) to produce summary data.

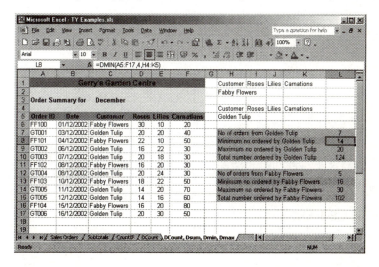

Summary

This chapter has discussed how you work with a list of entries in an Excel worksheet using database type features. We have considered:

- Database terminology and how it relates to Excel terminology.
- Sorting rows into ascending or descending order using a simple sort.
- Multi-level sorts.
- Using Sort to rearrange columns.
- Locating data using the AutoFilter.
- Locating data using the Advanced Filter.
- Validation rules.
- Displaying your list as a simple form.
- Subtotals.
- Database functions.

10 macros

In this unit you will learn

- what macros are
- how to record, run, edit and delete macros
- about making your macros available to all workbooks

Aims of this chapter

We have already discussed some of the features that can be used to help you automate the way you work in Excel – AutoFormat, Styles, Templates, etc. In this chapter we will consider how macros can help you automate your work. Macros are useful when you want to automate a routine that you perform regularly. We will look at some examples where you may find macros useful. You will learn how to record, play back and edit the macros you create.

10.1 What are macros?

A macro is a set of Excel commands grouped together so that you can execute them as a single command.

If you perform a task often, but cannot find an Excel keyboard shortcut, or tool, that runs through the sequence you want to use, you should record the commands into a macro. You have then created a 'custom' command.

What could you use a macro for?

- Speeding up routine editing and formatting.
- Recording the instructions to create a new document using one of your own templates, e.g. your budget or monthly sales figures.
- Quickly accessing an option in a dialog box that you regularly use.
- Combining a group of commands you often execute in the same sequence.

There are two ways to create macros in Excel:

- **Recording** – we will be using this option. You can record any function that you can access through the menus and dialog boxes.
- **Visual Basic Editor** – you can record powerful, flexible macros using this. These macros can include Visual Basic as well as Excel commands. We will take a brief excursion into the Editor when we discuss editing macros.

10.2 Recording your macro

Before you start recording your macro, think through what it is that you want to record. If there are any commands that you're not sure about, try them out first to check that they do what you want to record.

Try recording a simple macro that creates a new workbook using one of your own templates.

To create your new workbook, you must:

1 Choose **New** from the **File** menu
2 Click **General Templates...** on the **Task Pane**
3 Select your template from the **General** tab
4 Click **OK**

The next example uses the template set up in Chapter 8.

To record the macro:

1 Open the **Tools** menu, choose **Macro** then **Record New Macro...**
2 Give your macro a name – something like *MyTemplate* would be appropriate
- Don't use spaces in the macro name – most of the punctuation characters are also not allowed.

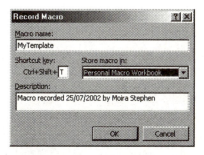

- If you want to separate words, use the underline character.
3 If you want a keyboard shortcut, click in the **Shortcut** field and enter the shortcut you want to use, e.g. **Ctrl+Shift+T**
4 Select the workbook you want to store the macro in

- If you choose the Personal Macro Workbook, your macro will be globally available, in every workbook you create.
5 Click **OK**
- You will be returned to your worksheet, and the **Stop Recording** toolbar will be displayed.
6 Work through the steps you want to record
7 Click the **Stop** tool on the Stop Recording toolbar when you've finished
- If the Stop Recording toolbar is not displayed, you can stop by opening the **Tools** menu, choosing **Macro** and then **Stop Recording**.

10.3 Playing back your macro

You can play back a macro with the keyboard shortcut, if you created one, or through the Tools menu.

To use the keyboard shortcut:

- Press the keyboard shortcut key sequence you recorded, e.g. **Ctrl+Shift+T** to create your new workbook.

To use the Tools menu:

1 Open the **Tools** menu and choose **Macro**
2 Select **Macros...**
3 At the **Macro** dialog box, select the macro you want to play back and click **Run**

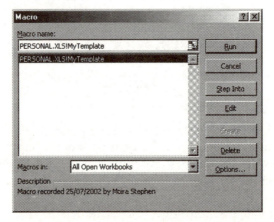

The given example is a simple one to illustrate how a macro can be recorded and executed. You will find that macros are especially useful when you have long sequences of commands to work through.

10.4 Ideas for more macros

You can record almost anything you want into a macro. Some of the things that you could record into a macro may also be automated in other ways, e.g. AutoFormat or Styles. Macros are usually used to carry out a sequence of commands.

If you find that you regularly use a series of commands in the same order, or use an option that is buried deep in a dialog box, macros can help you speed up the way you work.

Try out the following macros to get some more practice. They are all easy to set up.

Setting up a Header and/or Footer

If you use the same header and/or footer in many of your workbooks, you could record the sequence of commands into a macro.

1 Open the **Tools** menu, choose **Macro** then **Record New Macro...**
2 Give your macro a name – *HeaderFooter* or something similar
3 If you want a keyboard shortcut, click in the **Shortcut** field and enter the shortcut, e.g. **Ctrl+Shift+F**
4 Select the workbook you want to store the macro in – store it in the Personal Macro Workbook if you want it to be available to all workbooks
5 Click **OK**. You will be returned to your worksheet, and the Stop Recording toolbar will be displayed
6 Open the **File** menu and choose **Page Setup...**
7 Select the **Header/Footer** tab
8 Set up the header and/or footer as required
9 Click **OK**
10 Click the **Stop** tool when you've finished

Discount calculator

Let's say you offer a discount to your customers based on the amount of their order. You could record a simple discount calculator into a macro, then access the calculator from any workbook. This macro will:

1 Create a new blank worksheet within your workbook
2 Enter the text and formula to the discount calculator
3 Protect the sheet so that only the *Amount of Order* details can be entered

Try it out!

1 Create a new workbook, or open an existing one
2 Start to record a new macro
3 Give your macro a name – *DiscountCal* or something similar – and enter a keyboard shortcut if you want one
4 Select the workbook you want to store the macro in
5 Click **OK**
6 Insert a new worksheet – open the **Insert** menu and choose **Worksheet**
7 Enter the text and the formula to calculate the discount (in this example 7.5%) and balance due (see below – don't display the formulas)
8 Format the cells to **Currency**

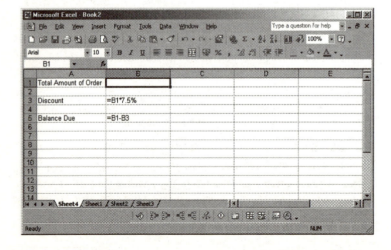

9 Unlock the cell that will take the *Amount of order* and protect the worksheet (see section 5.9)

10 Stop recording

If you recorded the macro in your Personal Macro Workbook, you can access it from anywhere using the keyboard shortcut, or run the macro from the Macro dialog box.

10.5 Deleting a macro

As you experiment with setting up macros, you will inevitably end up with some that you don't want to keep. They may not prove as useful as you first thought, or they might not run properly. You can delete any macro you no longer require.

If the macro you want to delete is in the Personal Macro Workbook, you must 'unhide' the workbook before you can delete it.

To unhide the Personal Macro Workbook:

1 Open the **Window** menu and choose **Unhide...**
2 Select the workbook – *Personal* in this case
3 Click **OK**

To delete a macro:

1 Open the **Tools** menu and select **Macro**
2 Choose **Macros...**
3 Select the macro you want to delete from the list displayed
4 Click **Delete**

5 Confirm the deletion at the prompt

If you have displayed your Personal Macro Workbook, you must hide it again once you've deleted any macros you don't want to keep. Do not close it – if you do you won't be able to use the macros that you recorded in the workbook.

To hide the Personal Macro Workbook again:

- Open the **Window** menu and choose **Hide**.

If you accidentally close the Personal Macro Workbook, you can open it again using the **Open** command on the **File** menu. If you have Excel installed on your C drive, the Personal Macro Workbook can be found in C:\Program Files\Microsoft Office\Office\XLstart.

10.6 Editing a macro

I'd suggest you re-record any short macro that has an error in it rather than try to edit it – it will probably be quicker. However, if you have recorded a longer macro or have a minor adjustment to make, it may be quicker to edit it rather than re-record the whole thing.

The macros you record are translated into Visual Basic – so things may look a bit strange when you first try editing a macro. But don't worry, if you take your time and have a look through the instructions you'll soon be able to relate your actions in Excel to the Visual Basic code.

When editing a macro, be very careful not to delete anything you don't understand, or insert anything that should not be there – you might find your macro no longer runs properly if you do.

If the worst comes to the worst and the macro stops working, you can always record it again.

The Visual Basic code will often have far more lines of code than the number of commands you intentionally recorded. Don't worry about this – some instructions are picked up from default settings in dialog boxes. Just scroll through until you see something you recognize as the line you want to change.

Let's try editing the discount amount in our discount calculator to make it 12.5%.

If the discount calculator macro is in the Personal Macro Workbook, you must unhide the workbook before you can edit it.

To edit the macro:

1. Open the **Tools** menu and choose **Macro** then **Macros...**
2. Select the macro you wish to edit

3 Click the **Edit** button
- The Visual Basic code for the macro will be displayed.
4 Scroll through the code to find the area you want to change
5 Edit as required
6 Save the changes – click the **Save** tool on the Standard toolbar
7 Close – click the **Close** button on the Microsoft Visual Basic title bar

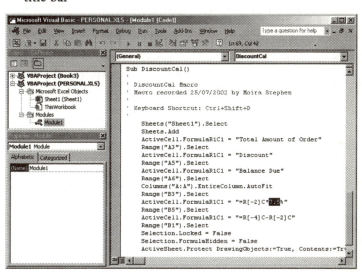

10.7 Saving macros on exit

If you have saved some macros into your Personal Macro Workbook, a prompt will appear when you exit Excel, asking if you want to save the changes to that workbook. If you want to be able to use the macros you have created the next time you use Excel, click **Yes** at the prompt.

Summary

In this chapter we have discussed macros. You have learnt how to:

- Record a macro using the Macro Recorder.
- Give the macro a keyboard shortcut.
- Run the macro.
- Delete a macro.
- Edit a macro using the Visual Basic Editor.
- Save the changes to the Personal Macro Workbook so that you can use them again the next time you use Excel.

toolbars

In this unit you will learn

- about working with toolbars
- how to manipulate and customize toolbars
- how to assign macros to tools

Aims of this chapter

In this chapter we discuss toolbars. We'll look at basic toolbar manipulation – the positioning of toolbars, and showing and hiding them. We'll also discuss how you can edit toolbars, create new ones and assign macros to them. Finally, we'll discuss some of the other options available when working with toolbars, including how to modify the image on a tool.

11.1 Standard and Formatting toolbars

When working in Excel the Standard toolbar and Formatting toolbar normally share a row along the top of your screen. If you prefer to give these toolbars a row each, you can switch the row-sharing option off.

To toggle row-sharing for the Standard and Formatting toolbar:

1 Right-click on a toolbar
2 Choose **Customize...** from the list
3 Select the **Options** tab
4 Select or deselect **Show Standard and Formatting toolbars on two rows**

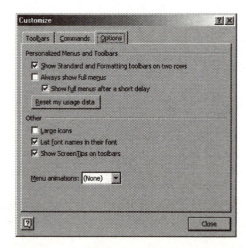

Other options on this tab let you control how the menus work

Or

5 Click the Toolbar options button (drop-down arrow at right edge of toolbar) and click **Show Buttons on One Row/Show Buttons on Two Rows**

11.2 Moving toolbars

Toolbars can be positioned *anywhere* on your screen. There are four *docking* areas – at the top, bottom, left and right of the Excel window frame. You can also leave your toolbar *floating* anywhere on the screen.

To move a toolbar if it is docked

1 Point to the raised line at the left edge of the toolbar (if it is docked at the top or bottom of the screen) or top edge (if it is docked at the left or right)
2 Drag and drop the toolbar into its new position

To move a toolbar if it is not docked

1 Point to its Title bar
2 Drag and drop the toolbar into its new position

11.3 Showing and hiding toolbars

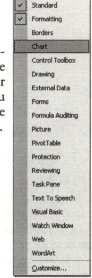

You will have noticed that some toolbars appear and disappear automatically when you are working in Excel. You can also opt to show or hide toolbars whenever you wish. Provided you have at least one toolbar displayed, you can use the shortcut method to show or hide toolbars.

To use the shortcut method:

1 Point to a toolbar
2 Click the *right* mouse button
• Any toolbars that are already displayed have a tick beside their name.
3 Click (using the *left* mouse button) on the toolbar name that you wish to show or hide

If no toolbars are displayed, you must use the **View** menu to show them again.

1. Open the **View** menu and choose **Toolbars**
2. Click on the one you want to show

Using either of the methods above, you can show or hide one toolbar at a time. If you want to change the display status of several toolbars at the one time, it may be quicker to use the **Customize** dialog box.

1. Right-click on a toolbar that is currently displayed

Or

2. Open the **View** menu and choose **Toolbars**.
- Click **Customize...**
3. Select or deselect the toolbars in the list as required
4. Click **Close**

Toolbars are useful, but the more you have on screen, the less you can see of your worksheet!

11.4 Editing existing toolbars

If you find that there are some tools on a toolbar that you tend not to use, or if you want to add another tool to a toolbar, you can edit the toolbar. If you want to add several tools to a toolbar, you should create a new toolbar and add your tools to it – see section 11.5. If you want to edit a toolbar it must be displayed.

To edit an existing toolbar:

1 Display the toolbar you want to edit
2 Click the **Toolbar Options** drop-down arrow to the right of the toolbar
3 Place the mouse pointer over **Add or Remove Buttons**
4 Point to the toolbar name
5 Select or deselect the tools as required

Or

6 If the tool is not displayed, click **Customize** to open the **Customize** dialog box
7 Select the **Commands** tab

You can also open the Customize dialog box through the View menu (see page 184). In this dialog box, you can add tools to, remove them from, or move them around on a toolbar.

To add a tool:

1 Select the **Category** of tool you're looking for
2 Locate the tool in the **Commands** list
3 Drag it over to the toolbar – when you are over a toolbar a very dark I-beam with a + beside it indicates your position – and drop it into position (if you are not over a toolbar, the mouse pointer has a small button with an **x**)

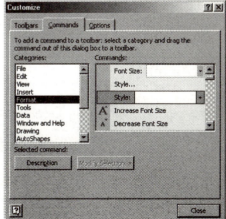

If you want a brief description of a tool's purpose, select it in the list of commands on the **Commands** tab, or on the toolbar, then click the **Description** button.

To move a tool:

1 With the **Customize** dialog box open, drag the tool to the correct position on the toolbar
2 Drop it

To remove a tool:

1 With the **Customize** dialog box open, drag the tool off the toolbar
2 Drop it anywhere
3 Click **Close** in the **Customize** dialog box when you've finished editing your toolbar

The drop-down list tools that appear on toolbars, e.g. Style and Font on the Formatting toolbar take up a lot more room than one of the smaller buttons.

If you need to free up some space on a toolbar that contains drop-down tools, you can change the size of these tools as required.

To change the size of a drop-down tool:

1 Open the **Customize** dialog box
2 On the appropriate toolbar, select the tool you want to resize e.g. `Currency [0]`
3 Click and drag the right or left edge of it – the mouse pointer becomes a thick double-headed arrow when you are in the correct place

Shortcut

You can quickly move or delete tools from a toolbar that is displayed *without* opening the Customize dialog box.

To move a tool: Hold down the **[Alt]** key and drag the tool along the toolbar (or to another toolbar).

To delete a tool: Hold down the **[Alt]** key and drag the tool off the toolbar.

11.5 Creating a new toolbar

If you have several tools that you'd like to add to a toolbar (or macros to assign to tools), you may need to create a new toolbar, rather than try to squeeze tools into the existing ones.

To create a new toolbar:

1 Open the **Customize** dialog box
2 Select the **Toolbars** tab
3 Click **New...**
4 Give your toolbar a name and click **OK**

5 Your toolbar will be displayed
6 Choose the **Commands** tab and add the tools you require to your new toolbar (see section 11.4)
7 Close the **Customize** dialog box

11.6 Adding your macros to toolbars

In Chapter 10 we discussed macros. The ones you set up can be assigned to a tool on a toolbar, and run with a simple click!

To assign a macro to a toolbar:

1 Display the toolbar you want to assign your macro to
2 Open the **Customize** dialog box

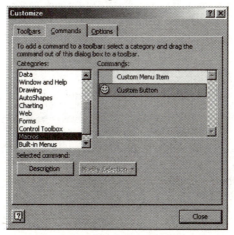

3 Choose the **Commands** tab
4 Select the **Macros** category
5 Drag the Custom Button over onto your toolbar
6 Right-click on the tool on your toolbar and click **Assign Macro...**
7 Select the macro you want to assign to the macro button
8 Click **OK**
9 Close the **Customize** dialog box

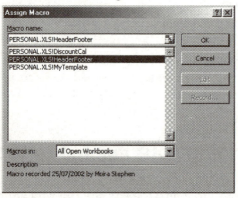

11.7 Change the button image and name

You may want to change the custom button image – things get a bit confusing if you use the same one for several macros! If you are assigning several macros to tools on a toolbar, you don't want them all with a smiley face!

To change the button image:

1 Display the toolbar that has the macro button image on it
2 Open the **Customize** dialog box and select the **Commands** tab
3 Select the macro button on your toolbar
4 Click **Modify Selection**
5 Choose **Change Button Image**
6 Select an image for your macro button

The Screen Tip (see section 1.8) that appears when you point to a custom button is taken from the **Name** field in the **Modify Selection** list.

To display a message that reflects its purpose:

1 Follow steps 1 to 4 as above
2 Select the text '*&Custom Button*' that appears in the **Name:** field
3 Type in the text you want to display
4 Click anywhere off the list to close it
5 Close the **Customize** dialog box when you've finished

11.8 Resetting toolbars

If you have modified one of the preset toolbars that come with Excel, then decide you want to set it back to how it was when you installed the package, you can restore its original settings.

To reset an Excel toolbar:

1 Click **Reset Toolbar** at the bottom of the **Add or Remove Buttons** list

Or

2 Open the **Customize** dialog box and select the **Toolbars** tab

3 Click on the toolbar you want to reset – it doesn't matter if the toolbar is displayed or not
4 Click the **Reset...** button
5 Respond to the prompt as appropriate – **OK** to reset the toolbar, **Cancel** if you've changed your mind

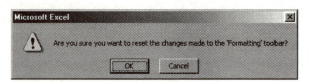

Summary

In this chapter we have discussed the various options available when working with and modifying toolbars. We have discussed:

- Positioning toolbars on your screen.
- Showing and hiding toolbars.
- Adding tools to toolbars.
- Moving tools on toolbars.
- Removing tools from toolbars.
- Creating new toolbars.
- Assigning macros to a toolbar.
- Changing the custom button image and name.
- Resetting an Excel toolbar.

12 excel with other applications

In this unit you will learn

- the difference between linking and embedding
- how to link data in other applications to Excel
- how to use Excel data in a Word Mail Merge

Aims of this chapter

Excel is part of the Microsoft Office suite, and it integrates very well with the other applications in the suite. If you have the complete suite then you have the benefit of being able to use the most appropriate tool for the job. This chapter discusses some of the ways in which the Office applications can be integrated.

12.1 Linking vs embedding

Linking and embedding are techniques that enable you exchange data between Excel and other applications. The key differences between linked and embedded data lie in where it is stored and how it is updated.

Linked data

Linked data *is not* stored in your Excel workbook. It is stored in a file, e.g. a document or presentation, in the source application (the one in which it was created). The data is updated within the source application – and those changes are reflected in the Excel workbook to which it is linked.

Advantages of linking data include:

- The Excel workbook is smaller than with embedded data.
- The data in the Excel workbook reflects the current status of the source data.

Embedded data

Embedded data *is* stored in your Excel workbook. However, when you create and edit the data, you have access to all the functions within the source application.

Advantages of embedding data:

- All the data is held in one file.
- You have access to powerful functions that are not part of the Excel application when creating and editing the object.

The following sections discuss some of the methods you can use to integrate the data across the applications in Office XP.

12.2 Copy and Paste

You can copy text, data, graphics, charts, etc. from one application to another within the Office XP suite using simple copy and paste techniques. We will consider how you can copy charts and data *from* Excel into other applications in the Office suite.

To copy and paste:

1 Start Excel *and* the application you want to copy the data or chart to
2 Open the workbook that you are copying from, and the file that will receive the copy
3 Select the chart or data you want to copy
4 Click the **Copy** tool on the Standard toolbar
5 Switch to the application you want to copy the data or chart into
6 Place the insertion point where you want the data or chart to appear
7 Click the **Paste** tool on the Standard toolbar

When you copy charts and data in this way, the chart or data is not 'linked' to the original data in the Excel workbook in any way. Should you edit the data in Excel, the data you copied into the destination file remains as it was when you copied it.

You can copy and paste data from Excel into a Word document, a PowerPoint presentation or an Access database. When you copy and paste data into these applications the data is displayed in a table in the destination application.

You can also copy and paste charts from Excel into a Word document or a PowerPoint presentation.

12.3 Linking data

If you want the data that you copy into your file to be kept in line with the data held in Excel, you should create a link to it. You can use the Paste options or Copy and Paste Special to create a link.

To link data:

1. Start Excel *and* the application you want to copy data to
2. Select the chart or data you want to copy
3. Click the **Copy** tool on the Standard toolbar
4. Switch to the application you want to copy into
5. Place the insertion point where you want the chart or data to appear
6. Paste the data using the **Paste** tool
7. Click the **Paste options** button
8. Choose a link option

Or

9. Open the **Edit** menu and choose **Paste Special**
10. Select the **Paste Link** button
11. Choose an option from the **As:** list – when you select an option a brief description of how it works appears in the Result box
12. Click **OK**

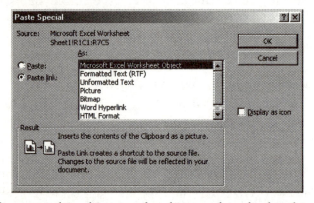

When copied in this way, the chart or data displayed in the destination file is linked to the original data in Excel. Should you edit the data in the Excel, it will be updated automatically in your Word document or PowerPoint presentation.

12.4 Embedding data

You can copy and paste, or use Paste Special to get data or charts from Excel into a document in Word or PowerPoint. However, if you want data in Word or PowerPoint, and it isn't already set up in Excel (and doesn't need to be), you can insert a worksheet into a Word or PowerPoint file. It will be created and edited using Excel functions.

The Excel Worksheet you insert will be an embedded object.

To insert a Microsoft Excel Worksheet:

1 Place the insertion point where you want the worksheet to appear in your Word document or PowerPoint presentation
2 Click the **Insert Microsoft Excel Worksheet** tool on the Standard toolbar
3 Click and drag over the grid to specify the worksheet size

♦ You end up with an embedded worksheet, with the toolbars and menus of Excel displayed.
4 Set up your worksheet as normal
5 Click anywhere outside the worksheet area when you've finished to return to your Word or PowerPoint document
♦ To edit your worksheet, double-click on it – you will be returned to Excel.

12.5 Mail Merge

Data in an Excel workbook can be used in a Mail Merge in Word. The workbook is used as the Data Document in the merge.

From the worksheets that have been set up in this book, the student results worksheet could be merged into a Word document so that we could send letters out to our students telling them how well they had done in their exams. You could add columns to contain the student address details to the worksheet.

The top row of your data should contain the field names. Enter the data that will be merged into your document on the worksheet starting under the field name row.

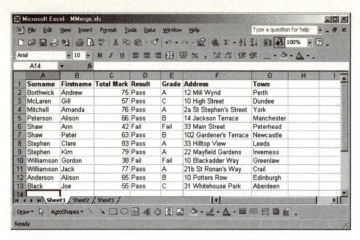

In Word, set up your Mail Merge document in the normal way. Select your Excel workbook and open your DataSource.

Choose the sheet required, or select the named range that contains the data you wish to use.

Complete the Main Document in Word using the fields from your worksheet.

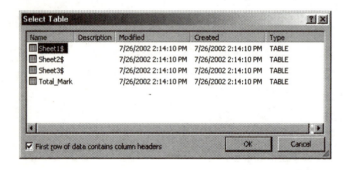

Summary

In this chapter we have discussed some of the ways you can integrate Excel with the rest of the Microsoft Office suite. We have considered:

- The difference between linking and embedding data.
- Copy and Paste.
- Linking the source data in an Excel workbook with the copy in Word or PowerPoint using *Copy and Paste Special*.
- Embedding a worksheet in Word and in PowerPoint.
- Merging an Excel list into a Word Mail Merge document.

13
excel and the web

In this unit you will learn

- how to send your workbooks by e-mail
- about hyperlinks
- how to set up your data on Web pages

Aims of this chapter

This chapter discusses using Excel with the wider world. You will learn how to e-mail an Excel workbook. You will also learn how to use hyperlinks to link to other files on your own computer or network, and to pages on the World Wide Web. Finally, we'll create a Web document from within Excel and discuss how to publish it to the Web. The examples in this chapter are based on the use of Outlook Express for e-mail. You must also have access to the Internet, and be familiar with its basics, for this chapter.

13.1 E-mail

Provided you have a modem, communications software and a service provider, you can e-mail your Excel workbook to anywhere in the world. E-mail is usually very fast – sometimes your message will be delivered almost instantly, other times it may take an hour or so.

You can e-mail an open workbook directly from Excel. The whole workbook can be sent as a file 'attachment' to the message or the current worksheet can be sent, as text, as the body of the message – though this option is only available if Outlook or Outlook Express is your default e-mail application.

To e-mail a workbook from within Excel:

1 Open the workbook you want to e-mail
2 Click the **E-mail** tool
3 Select the option required and click **OK**

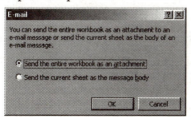

4 Enter the e-mail address you want to send the message to (or open the Address Book and select it from the list)

5 Enter or edit the subject as necessary
6 Type in your message
7 Click **Send** (if you opted to send the whole workbook) or **Send this sheet** (if you opted to send the current sheet)

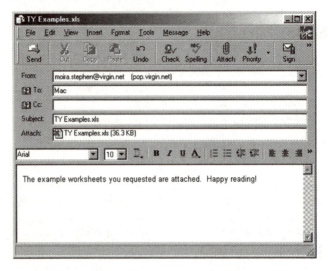

To attach a workbook from within your mail software:

1 Click the **Create a New Mail Message** tool
2 Enter the address in the **To** field and **Cc** field if necessary
3 Type in your subject
4 Key in your message

To attach a file:

5 Click the **Attach** tool
6 Select the file you want to attach and click **Attach** in the open file dialog box
7 Repeat steps 5–6 if you want more than one file attached
8 Send your message

13.2 Hyperlinks

A hyperlink is a 'hot spot' that lets you jump from your workbook to another location – on your own computer, on your company network or anywhere in world via the Internet.

Adding hyperlinks

You can insert a hyperlink anywhere in your workbook. When you click one, the file that it points to is displayed on screen.

To insert a hyperlink to a file on your system:

1 Select the cell you want to place your hyperlink in

2 Click the **Insert Hyperlink** tool on the Standard toolbar

3 Locate the file on your system

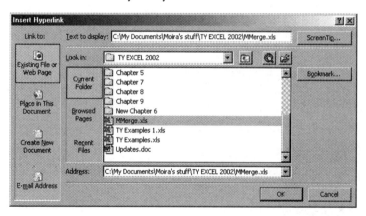

4 Click **OK**

The hyperlink will be inserted into your workbook. The text usually appears blue, with a blue underline.

To insert a hyperlink to a place within the workbook:

1 Select the cell for the hyperlink and click

2 If you have a named location in your file, e.g. a sheet name or named range in a workbook, or a bookmark in a document, click Bookmark... to open the dialog box to help you specify the location required

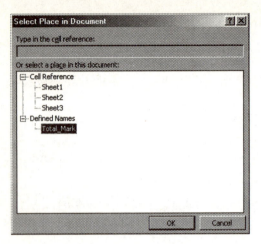

You can jump to a named place or to a cell reference on a selected sheet in your workbook

3 Select a sheet and enter the cell range required, or select the named range required from the **Defined Names** list

4 Click **OK** to return to the **Insert Hyperlink** dialog box

5 Click **OK**

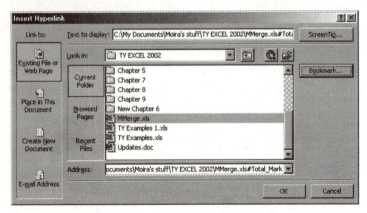

To insert a hyperlink to a URL on the Web:

1 Select the cell for the hyperlink and click

2 Type in the URL (Uniform Resource Locator – the Internet address) of the file you want to jump to

Or

3 Click and browse the Web

4 Locate the page you want to link to
5 Return to Excel – click **Microsoft Excel** on the Task bar
6 Click **OK** at the **Insert Hyperlink** dialog box
- You can edit the contents of the **Text to display** field when inserting your hyperlink to get a user-friendly prompt in a cell, rather than the full URL.

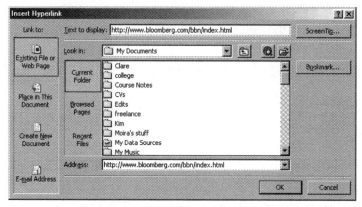

If you didn't enter a user-friendlier prompt in the Text to display field when setting up your hyperlink (or if you want to change a URL or bookmark) you can edit the hyperlink as necessary.

To edit a hyperlink:

1 Right-click on the cell that contains the hyperlink you wish to edit
2 Select **Edit Hyperlink...** from the menu
3 Edit the hyperlink details as required, e.g. enter the text you want to display in place of the URL in the **Text to display** field
4 Click **OK**

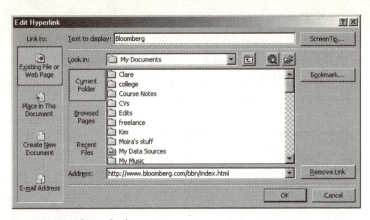

To remove a hyperlink:

1 Right-click on the cell that contains the hyperlink
2 Select **Remove Hyperlink**

Using hyperlinks

To jump to a hyperlink location:

1 Point to the hyperlink – the mouse pointer becomes a hand with a pointing finger – and click

When you jump to a file using a hyperlink, the **Web** toolbar is displayed.

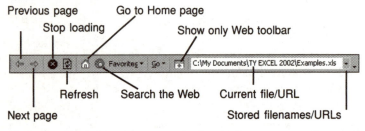

If the toolbar doesn't appear, right-click on any toolbar and choose **Web** from the list.

- To return to the workbook you jumped from, click the Excel button on the Taskbar.

Once you've jumped to a hyperlink, then returned to your workbook, the hyperlink field changes colour – usually to violet. This will remind you that you've already used that hyperlink.

13.3 Preparing a Web page

The pages you access through the Internet are part of the World Wide Web. You can create your own pages from Excel and publish them on the Web if you wish.

* To see how your workbook would look if you published it on the Web, open your workbook then choose **Web Page Preview** from the **File** menu.

Web pages published from Excel can be interactive or non-interactive. If the Web page is to be viewed, but not manipulated by the viewer, don't make the Web page interactive. If you want to allow users to interact with the data on your Web page, e.g. sort or filter it, you can make the Web page interactive. Both options are discussed below.

* Make sure you save your workbook as usual before you create a Web page from any part of it. You can then go back to the original workbook if necessary.

To prepare a page for the Web you must save it in a Web Page file.

To save a Web Page:

1 Open the workbook you want to prepare for publication
2 Choose **Save as Web Page...** from the **File** menu
3 Click **Publish**

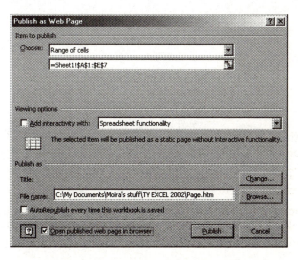

4 Select the data you wish to publish in the **Choose** field (or select *Range of Cells* and specify the range of cells)
5 Select/deselect the **Add interactivity with** checkbox as required
6 If you wish to enter a **Title** at the top of your published page, click **Change**, enter the title you want to use in the **Set Title** dialog box and click **OK**
7 Specify the path and file name for your file
8 To preview the page, select the *Open published web page in browser* checkbox
9 Click **Publish**

♦ A Web file, e.g. Page.htm, will be saved in the location specified in the **File name** field and the page will appear on your screen.

A non-interactive page can be viewed on the Web, but not manipulated. An interactive Web page displays a toolbar that can be used to manipulate the data on the Web page. You can sort, filter, copy and paste, etc. on an interactive page. Changes made to the page are not saved. Each time the page is accessed it will be displayed as it was originally set up.

♦ Close your Web browser when you've finished viewing your page.

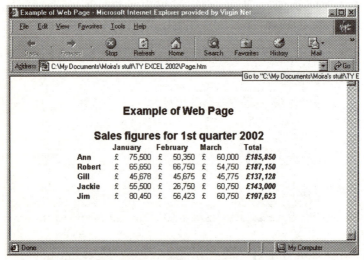

A non-interactive Excel Web page.

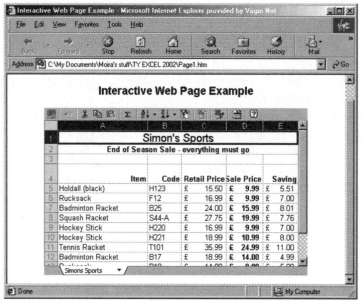

An interactive Web page – note the tools available to the reader.

13.4 Editing your Web page

Once you've set up your Web page you can update it if necessary.

If you want to update the workbook on which the Web page is based and the Web page, open the workbook, edit as necessary, save the workbook in the usual way, then repeat steps 2–9 on pages 205–206.

Choose **Replace File** at the prompt to replace an item that has already been published, select *Previously Published items* in the **Choose** field, then the item from the list that you wish to update.

If you want to edit a non-interactive Web page, but not the original workbook, open the Web page file itself.

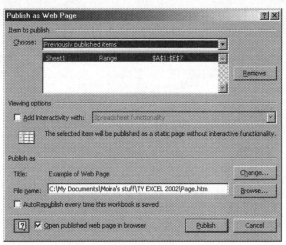

To edit a non-interactive Web page:

1 Open the Web page file in Excel – go to the **Open** dialog box, select the file and click **Open**
2 Edit as necessary
3 Click **Save** and close your file

You can open a non-interactive Web page file in Excel or in your browser, from the **Open** dialog box. If you want to open the file in your browser to view it rather than edit it, click the **Open** button's drop-down arrow and choose **Open in Browser**.

To edit an interactive Web page:

If you have set up an interactive Web page you can edit it in Excel or a Web page editing application, e.g. FrontPage.

When you open an interactive Web page it is opened in your Web editor by default. If you wish to open it in Excel or your browser, click the **Open** drop-down arrow in the **Open** dialog box and select the option required.

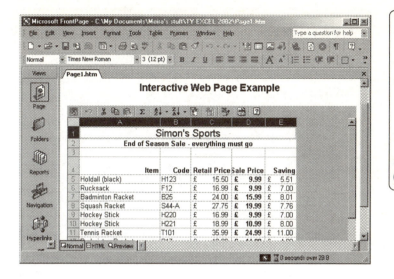

13.5 Publishing to the Web

To publish your Web page to the Web you must copy your file from your own computer to your service provider's server. This will be switched on 24 hours a day, so anyone who knows the URL of your Web page will be able to access it at any time.

You may have folders set up in My Network Places (on the Places bar in the Save As dialog box) for your files, or you could publish them to MSN.

Most service providers will allocate some free storage space to you for your own Web pages – 10 Mb (about 7 diskettes worth) is fairly typical.

There are a number of ways to upload files to a service provider's server – contact your service provider to find out how to upload your files to their server.

If you have created hyperlinks in your Web page that jump to other files on your computer, remember to upload all the files, not just the main page.

To keep your files on the Web up to date, remember to update them and copy the new versions to your service provider's server as necessary.

Summary

This final chapter has discussed ways in which you can interact with the wider world from Excel. We have covered how to:

- Send and receive e-mail messages.
- Create hyperlinks to other files, to places in a workbook and to Web pages.
- Display a user-friendly prompt for hyperlinks.
- Create interactive and non-interactive pages for publication to the Web.
- Edit Web files.
- Find out about publishing your Web pages.

taking it further

If you've mastered half of what's in this book, you are well on the way to becoming a proficient Excel user. If you are getting to grips with most of it, you are doing very well indeed.

You'll find lots of information on Excel on the Internet, in addition to the **Help** menu option **Office on the Web** that takes you to **http://office.microsoft.com/uk/assistance/**.

Other sites that you may find useful include:

http://www.microsoft.com/office/excel/default.asp

http://search.support.microsoft.com/search/

You could also try searching the Web for sites that provide information on Word. Try entering "Microsoft Excel" + "Software Reviews" into your search engine. You should come up with several sites worth a look.

If you would like to join a course to consolidate your skills, you could try your local college, or search the Internet for on-line courses. Most courses cost money, but you may find the odd free one – try:

http://www.baycongroup.com/wlesson0.htm

Good Excel skills are useful on many levels – personal, educational and vocational. Now that you have improved your Excel skills, why not consider going for certification? The challenge of an exam can be fun, and a recognized certificate may improve your job prospects. There are a number of different bodies that you could consider.

You may want to consider MOUS exams (Microsoft Office User Specialist) or ECDL (European Computer Driving Licence – basic or advanced) certification. Or, if you feel more ambitious, how about other Microsoft Certified Professional exams!

Visit **http://www.microsoft.com/traincert/mcp/mous/** for information on MOUS certification or **http://www.ecdl.com** for information on ECDL.

index

Absolute address 83
Active cell 23
Address, of cell 19
Alignment, within cells 48
AND 103
Answer Wizard 13
AutoFill 37
AutoFilter 158
AutoFit 30
AutoFormat 145
AutoShapes 140
AutoSum 72

Bold 47
Borders 50
Bring Forward 141
Button image 188

Callouts 140
Cell 18
Cell name 19
Cell protection 93
Cell range 25
Chart
  data preparation 128
  default 136
  embedded 134
  objects 132
  managing 132
  printing 134
  special effects 136
  Wizard 129
Circular references 86, 158
Column 18
Column width

AutoFit 30
  change default 31
  manual adjustment 30
Comments 91
Comparison operators 98
Concatenate 108
Conditional formatting 53
Converting cell addresses to named ranges 90
Copy and Paste 41
  between applications 193
COUNTIF 106
Currency format 33
Cut & Paste 40

Data entry 27
Data editing 28
Data form 164
Data tables 117
Data validation 162
Database functions 168
Database terminology 154
DAY 111
DCOUNT 168
Default font, change 54
Delete
  cell contents 28
  row or column 42
DMAX 169
DMIN 168
Docking areas 183
Drag & Drop 41
Drawing objects 138
Drawing tools 138
DSUM 169

E-mail 199
Edit cell contents 28
Embedded data 192
Entering data 27
Exit Excel 97 16

Filter, Advanced 161
Financial functions 113
Flip 142
Font setting 49
Footers 60
Format Cells dialog box 51
Format Data Series 137
Format Painter 52
Formatting toolbar 182
Formula Auditing toolbar 81
Formulas 19, 34
Freeze panes 55
Functions 19
  database 168
  date 110
  financial 113
  inserting 76
  logical 97
  lookup 115
  statistical and math 106
  text 107
FV 115

Gridlines, printing 61
Grouping objects 140

Headers 60
Help
  Answer Wizard 13
  Contents Tab 12
  Dialog Box 14
  Index Tab 13
  Office Assistant 8
  Screen Tips 14
  What's This? 11
HLOOKUP 115
Hyperlink 201

IF function 97
  nested 100
Insert column 42
Insert row 42
Italic 47

Iterations 87

Jargon 18

Keyboard shortcuts 47

Linked data 192
Lookup functions 115
LOWER 109

Macros 172
  adding to toolbars 187
  deleting 177
  editing 178
  play back 174
  recording 173
  saving 179
Mail merge 195
Margins 58
Menus, using the keyboard 8
MONTH 111
Moving around a worksheet,
  using the mouse 25

Name box 23
Named range
  create 88
  delete 89
Named ranges 87
NOW() 111
NPV 115
Number formats 33
Numeric data 19

Office Assistant 8
  Customize 10
  Tips 10
Open workbook 20
Operators 35
OR 104
Order of precedence 36
Orientation 57
Outline pane 167

Page breaks 59
Page layout 57
Page order 62
Page size 58
Parentheses 36
Password protection 22

Paste Special 193
Personal Macro Workbook 174
   hide/unhide 177
   open 178
   save changes 179
PivotTable 122
PMT 114
Precedence, in calculations 36
Print 44
   gridlines 61
   part of a worksheet 44
   row and column headings 61
Print Preview 43
PROPER 110
Publishing to the Web 209
PV 114

RATE 114
Relative address 38, 82
Replace cell contents 28
Rotate 142
Row 18

Save As 22
Save workbook 21
Scaling 58
Scenarios 120
Selection techniques 24
Send Backward 141
Sheet tab 64
Shrink to fit 33
Sort 155
   columns 157
Split box 56
Split screen 56
Standard toolbar 182
Starting Excel 97
   Shortcut Bar 4
Styles 146
   apply 146
   delete 147
   edit 147
Subtotals 166
SUMIF 107

Tab split box 64
Templates
   workbook 148
   worksheet 151

Text box 140
Text entries 19
Text functions 107
Text wrap within a cell 31
TODAY() 111
Toolbars 6
   assign macro 187
   Chart 131
   Circular Reference 86
   Drawing 138
   Formatting 6
   Formula Auditing 81
   modify 184
   move 182
   new 187
   Print Preview 43
   Reviewing 93
   show/hide 183
   Standard 6
   Web 204

Underline 47
UPPER 108

Validation rules 162
View formula 80
Visual Basic code 178
Visual Basic Editor 172
VLOOKUP 116

Web page
   editing 206
   interactive 206
   preparing 205
Wizards 131
Workbook templates 148
Worksheet
   copying 68
   deleting 67
   design 64
   grouping 69
   inserting 66
   moving 68
   moving between 64
   protection 93
   renaming 68
   templates 151

YEAR 111